Learning Circles

Creating Conditions for Professional Development

- Michelle Collay

- Diane Dunlap

- Walter Enloe

- George W. Gagnon Jr.

CORWIN PRESS, INC.
A Sage Publications Company
Thousand Oaks, California

For information:

Corwin Press, Inc.
A Sage Publications Company
2455 Teller Road
Thousand Oaks, California 91320
E-mail: order@corwinpress.com

SAGE Publications Ltd.
6 Bonhill Street
London EC2A 4PU
United Kingdom

SAGE Publications India Pvt. Ltd.
M-32 Market
Greater Kailash I
New Delhi 110 048 India

Printed in the United States of America

Library of Congress Cataloging-in-Publication Data

Main entry under title:

Learning circles: Creating conditions for professional development
/ by Michelle Collay ... [et al.].
   p. cm.
  Includes bibliographical references and index.
  ISBN 0-8039-6675-X (cloth: acid-free paper)
  ISBN 0-8039-6676-8 (pbk.: acid-free paper) 1.
  Group work in education—United States. 2.
Cooperativeness—United States. 3. Teachers—In-service
training—United States. 4. Teaching—United States. I. Collay,
Michelle.
  LB1032 .L355 1998
  370'.71'1—ddc21   98-9058

This book is printed on acid-free paper.

98 99 00 01 02 03 10 9 8 7 6 5 4 3 2 1

Editorial Assistant: Kristen L. Gibson
Production Editor: Diana E. Axelsen
Editorial Assistant: Denise Santoyo
Typesetter/Designer: Rebecca Evans/Lynn Miyata
Cover Designer: Tracy Miller

CONTENTS

Foreword   ix
   by Linda Lambert

Preface   xiii

   Professional Development and Communities
      of Learners   xiv
   Discovering the Power of Learning Circles   xv
   How This Book Is Organized   xvii
   Chapter Previews   xx
   Who Should Read This Book?   xxi
   Acknowledgments   xxii

About the Authors   xxiv

1. Creating Conditions   **1**

   What Are Learning Circles?   2
   Background of Our Thinking   3
   The Six Essential Conditions   8
   For Further Reading   12

2. Building Community   **13**

   What Is Community?   15
   Initiating Community   19
   Maintaining Community   22
   Sustaining Community   23
   Transforming Community   26
   Building Community Together   29
   For Further Reading   30

3. Constructing Knowledge   31

Knowing Naturally   32
Relating Whole and Parts   34
Designing Learning   35
Folding Paper   39
Playing Baby   42
Reinventing Kindergarten   43
Ways of Knowing   44
For Further Reading   46

4. Supporting Learners   47

Learning About Group Processes   49
Learning in Small Groups   51
Supporting Preservice Teachers   54
Supporting Professional Development   55
Supporting Teacher Research   57
For Further Reading   60

5. Documenting Reflection   62

Complex Systems   64
A Letter to Myself   64
Reflection on Stepping-Stones   67
Metaphor as Reflection   69
Journaling   72
Reflecting With Colleagues   73
Structured Reflection   74
Reflection for Program Evaluation   76
Reflection Within Learning Circles   77
For Further Reading   78

6. Assessing Expectations   79

Beliefs About Assessment   81
Appropriate Assessment   82
Approaches to Assessment   84
Self-Assessment   85
Peer Assessment   87

Portfolio Assessment	89
Changing the Culture of Assessment	93
For Further Reading	94
7. Changing Cultures	**95**
Interdependent Networks and Cultures	96
Understanding Culture	97
Making Sense of Culture in Learning Circles	101
Learning About Cultures Through Artifacts	102
Learning About Cultures Through Dance	104
Learning About Cultures Through Acting	105
Mentoring Others About Culture	106
Cultural Assumptions About Leaders	108
Teaching as Leading	111
For Further Reading	113
8. Re-Creating Conditions	**114**
Reconstructing Learning Circles	116
Practical Considerations	118
Variations on a Theme	121
Re-creating Conditions in Classrooms	123
Re-creating Conditions in Schools or Districts	127
Where From Here?	128
Conclusion	130
References	133
Index	137

FOREWORD

What does it mean to teach? I am reminded of Susan Loucks-Horsley's findings on "stuck," static schools compared with schools that were "unstuck," on the move. In the former schools, teachers reported that they believed that it took just three years to learn to teach. Not surprisingly, teachers in the latter schools reported that they believed it took a lifetime. The authors of this amazing book describe the journey of those lifetime learners. Even more captivating, they describe what that journey can look like from its theoretical inception to its practical conditions and strategies. The authors have "raised the bar" on what it means to teach.

Groups that learn together are not unique. Schools and universities, businesses, and agencies of all kinds use group work. What is unique about the "learning circles" described here is that the authors have discovered what makes such groups work. And they share their discoveries with us. Learning circles, as described by Collay, Dunlap, Enloe, and Gagnon, are "small communities of learners among teachers and others who come together intentionally for the purpose of supporting each other in the process of learning." The circles vary in membership and duration yet hold fast to intentionality, purpose, and learning. These circles capture the essence of interdependence found in natural ecological systems, especially those principles of flexibility, diversity of thought, energy flow, sustainability, and co-evolution or learning together. Capra points out that the purpose of life is learning—and that learning is constructivist for all living systems.

This work draws from a rich and diverse theoretical base that includes genetics, epistemology, natural sciences, psychology, and sociology. Into this theoretical primordial stew, the authors stir experience and *new* conceptions and interpretations. They emerge with six critical conditions for learning communities. These conditions, Building Community, Constructing Knowledge, Supporting Learners, Documenting Reflection, Assessing Expectations and Changing Cultures, are described in terms that readers should be able to use to begin their own learning circles or enrich their current learning groups.

Into the six conditions for learning circles, the authors have nested six learning conditions for children. Both the process and the content are constructivist. The authors offer an engaging template that involves feelings, images, and languages—all dimensions of the thoughts and expressions of learning. By reaching deeply into the experience of the child and through to the learning culture of an organization, the fractal is complete:

theorist → adult learner → child learner → organization learning.

Learning circle teachers have choice, take responsibility for their own development as professionals, and set their own agendas. As they explore and create these three freedoms (choice, responsibility, and agenda setting) together around shared work, they perform as a professional culture. As Newman and Wehlage have found, professional cultures that are directly related to student achievement have these four factors in place:

1. Shared decision making
2. A shared sense of purpose
3. Collaborative work toward that purpose
4. Collective responsibility

Teachers have been "out of the loop," particularly in regard to shared decision making. Although site-based management is in place in a perfunctory way in many regions of the country, teachers have yet to serve as major players in school reform. Teachers working in the kinds of cultures experienced in learning circles become activists by gaining access to their own power, their own energy.

Such an activist stance can enable teachers as a whole to push through the boundaries of full participation in schools. This process is the best hope for saving our schools.

Teacher preparation is under scrutiny as never before, and rightly so. Too many teacher educators still carry out archaic rounds: walking into school classrooms where a student teacher or intern is teaching, observing a lesson, giving lesson-specific feedback, and walking to their cars. This is important work indeed, but wholly inadequate. This singular focus neglects reflective practice and collegiality, school improvement, and the responsibility to influence others. The authors, in lifting the bar, thoroughly address the full range of teacher responsibilities.

Those who think a great deal about professional development have moved beyond inservice and training as the major framework for teacher learning in favor of opportunities to learn that involve collaboration, dialogue, reflection, inquiry, and leadership. However, the ancient paradigm is alive and well in schools. We find that our own graduate students interchange professional development and training automatically. This book should be required reading for teachers and administrators in preparation programs. If it were, we could anticipate a next generation of schools very different from those we have today.

Teachers represent the only significant educational group—and the largest one—that has not been held responsible for educational reform. To understand this imperative, it is essential to recognize that learning and leadership are inextricably intertwined. To lead is to engage community participants in the process of meaning making— the process of learning toward purpose. Most learning groups miss that essential element by focusing exclusively on the sacred duality in education: self-learning and child-learning. Professional learning has been centered on the self, teacher, and the child. While critically important, these two foci neglect the two that will change schools: responsibility for the learning of other adults in the culture and for the learning organization as a whole. The authors miss none of these nuances in their thoughtful perspective on learning and leading.

When I think about the making of this book, I have an image of four scholars sitting in Michelle and George's living room—their own learning circle—constructing and composing this book. The authors brought into that circle significant personal experiences, research backgrounds, and practical work. This is clearly a case of the whole being even greater than the sum of its parts. They have created a work that invokes their best thinking and creates new conceptions of learning. Piaget told us that "to understand is to invent." Collay, Dunlap, Enloe, and Gagnon truly understand.

Linda Lambert
California State University, Hayward

PREFACE

The four of us first met as colleagues who had a common interest in how people learn in community. We came together as a writing group to describe our learning experiences with teacher professional development. Based on our experience, we knew that most successful professional development occurs within supportive communities of learners. Many share this understanding of teacher learning. For instance, the fifth proposition of the National Board for Professional Teaching Standards (NBPTS, 1991) was developed primarily by master teachers. It states, "Teachers are members of learning communities." As our thinking evolved, we realized that healthy learning communities are made up of small supportive groups of learners. We called these groups *learning circles*.

As we told each other the stories of our professional lives, we realized that we had all had learning experiences in communities. Some of them were healthy, but others were not. We didn't recognize what was missing at the time, but we now know. We understand that most learning takes place within an individual but occurs through a process of a social interaction that creates conditions for personal transformation. Such change usually happens when a learner is **building community** with other learners who are **constructing knowledge** through their own experience and **supporting learners** involved with them in **documenting reflection** on their experiences and **assessing expectations** agreed on as they are **changing cultures** in their classrooms, institutions, workplaces, or organizations through their own actions. These six essential conditions are necessary for successful professional development experiences because they promote healthy communities of learners.

As we worked together on this book, we realized that our relatively swift agreement to use these six conditions had grown out of our individual but intersecting paths of professional development in many different learning situations. We now understand that our six guiding conditions are essential to all successful professional development. In fact, they are key indicators of readiness to conduct professional development and of whether a professional development learning event will be successful. Taken together, the six conditions are synergistic and create a whole that is greater than the sum of its parts, just as the whole of the human body is more than the sum of individual organs. Although a community might yield successful learning even if only three or four of the conditions are in place, it will always be more successful if all six are in place. In this book, we describe why these six conditions promote healthy communities of learners and how teachers can come together in learning circles to create conditions that support successful professional development.

PROFESSIONAL DEVELOPMENT AND COMMUNITIES OF LEARNERS

Throughout this book, we deliberately use the term "professional development" rather than "staff development" or "teacher in-service." Our intention is to convey the importance of acknowledging teachers as professionals engaged in their own development within the profession rather than viewing teachers as replaceable staff members who need to be trained or serviced. We are making a deliberate distinction between teacher "professional development" and "staff development" or "in-service." To us they are not the same thing. In-service and staff development are often done to teachers without their participation in planning or involvement in learning. It is something done for them by administrators who decide what they collectively need to know and pay little attention to what they individually want to learn. We should revisit the basic assumptions about learning and teaching in our current model for teacher professional development before attempting to prescribe wholesale educational reform. We advocate for teachers to engage in professional development with a small group of colleagues because of the support, reflection, and review this collective dialogue offers. We know, however, that professional development can be done by individual teachers who apply the ideas in this book to change their own classroom practice.

We also use the term *communities of learners* throughout this book. Communities of learners are groups of people gathered together intentionally for the purpose of supporting each other in the process of learning. These can be large groups of people who identify themselves as a community of learners, such as universities, colleges, or districts. *Community of learners* is a broad term that includes formal learning communities in university programs, college faculties, or K-12 schools as well as informal learning communities in courses for undergraduate or graduate students; in classrooms of secondary, elementary, or preschool students; and among different groups of teachers, students, administrators, business teams, church committees, organization boards, or others who are gathered together for the purpose of learning. The term can also refer to smaller groups of people in classrooms, schools, courses, or graduate programs. The smallest communities of learners are just a few people gathered together as grade-level teams, peer review groups, advisory groups, study groups, or site councils.

We are familiar with several communities of learners that became important examples for our own professional development: Vito Perrone's North Dakota Study Group on Evaluation, Bill Hull's Seminars on Children's Thinking, Eleanor Duckworth's Moon Group, Pat Carini's Children's Study Groups at New Prospect School, the Paideia School in Atlanta (not the Mortimer Adler Paideia Proposal), Dick Schmuck's Organization Development Cadres, Teachers Advocating Whole Language (TAWL), Jean Clandinen's Teacher Study Groups, and Sandra Hollingsworth's Literacy Groups. We appreciate their powerful contributions to our development as teachers and to the development of the ideas in this book.

DISCOVERING THE POWER
OF LEARNING CIRCLES

During the years we worked together in communities of learners, we realized that they worked best when leaders organized smaller groups of learners within the larger group. Members of small groups worked closely together providing community, support, review, feedback, and encouragement for each other as necessary. Small groups of learners can put into practice the six essential conditions more easily than a large group. The small groups provide a more personal forum for professional interaction and more opportunities for conversation where members can construct ideas together and people are more likely to share opinions and debate issues. Often, such small groups are formed around a specific topic or focus. These small groups within the larger group become the places where teachers first feel the power of belonging to a real community of learners. We realize the impact of small groups of teachers within the larger whole who provided continuity, thinking, support, reflection, feedback, and encouragement to change for one another—all the conditions we find important for creating healthy communities of learners. We now refer to small groups of teachers who are working together on their own professional development as learning circles.

Teachers in a learning circle emerged as leaders when the group focused on their agenda. There were no "anointed leaders" in a learning circle but a mutual reciprocity between the whole and its parts as all participants moved toward personal change and the common good. Individual autonomy within a democratic group process is vital to the success of learning circles. This sounds like a contradiction in terms but reflects our belief about decision making; any of us can choose to follow the rules of a particular event, but we are more likely to do so if we have been involved in making those rules ourselves and understand why they exist. We are better individual learners, group participants, and leaders of learning events when we experience supported learning ourselves. Our framework for this experience became a learning circle of individual teachers in a supportive group where the focus is on personal learning and professional development.

Learning circles provide a framework for individuals to change their practice and then influence the organizations in which they work. Although reform takes place one classroom at a time, the individuals making the change must have support from colleagues. Learning circles can provide that support. We are reminded of the advice of a beloved mentor: Reform is done *to* an organization, but organizations don't think or change; individuals do. Learning circles that offer support for individual teachers can then create a critical mass to influence the organization. Individuals also make meaning of the organization's structure or culture through membership in a learning circle. Listen to the level of engagement in a hall full of professionals when the "leader" asks the teachers to share ideas with a few others. They move instantly from passive receivers of information to makers of knowledge. This is the power of the small group or learning circle.

Some of our recent experiences offer precedents and working models for learning circles. We watched teachers in elementary and secondary classrooms form professional development groups with their grade-level or interdisciplinary team or department colleagues. They talked more about their own learning and teaching than about sports, politics, or personalities. We formed *teacher support teams* among university colleagues for peer review. These teacher support teams met monthly and took on similar characteristics to the small groups in the larger teacher communities. In a local district, some administrators met monthly in small groups over breakfast or lunch to compare notes and to discuss district policies. As we met regularly to write this book, we also found ourselves becoming what we were describing. We were a learning circle. Our ability to transcend considerable personal and professional trauma, differences in work schedules and life goals, and an unmovable deadline imposed by our lead author's pregnancy came from our use of the six conditions to create for ourselves the healthy learning circle we knew we could create for others. Our ability to remain friends and colleagues through a rough but worthwhile path of development was greatly aided by the conditions we had described for others. These six conditions, love, and great senses of humor carried the day. We use examples from our own experiences to inform our explanations throughout this work.

HOW THIS BOOK IS ORGANIZED

We offer an overview of the six essential conditions for creating healthy communities of learners in the first chapter, then provide a detailed description of each condition in separate chapters. The concluding chapter demonstrates how all six conditions interact and are essential for creating and recreating healthy learning circles and communities of learners. No conditions are sufficient alone or in combinations of two or three; they must all be in place. As we introduce a new condition in each chapter, we begin with our personal stories of how we arrived at an understanding of each process and the important role it plays in creating communities of learners. Then, we describe some theories we have used as the basis for deeper understanding and richer conceptualization of the condition. We end each chapter with illustrations and examples, typically lessons we designed, adapted, or borrowed and often experiences we had in communities of learners. We hope you will find these examples practical and clear enough to apply in your own learning circle. We have used teachers' voices to add credibility to our examples. These responses came from program evaluation documents; respondents' names were changed to pseudonyms to preserve anonymity.

Our stories of how we each arrived at an appreciation for what underlies healthy communities of learners is an important part of our journey to learning circles. We characterize these stories as "stepping-stones" in our journeys across the headwaters where communities of learners begin to flow into learning circles. We came together from very different parts of the world with very different educational paths. Through 2 years of daily and weekly conversations, we began to unearth what was in common across our experiences. Michelle Collay became aware of something other than classes as important places for learning when she was part of the band at a California high school. The band members became engaged in learning about themselves and what they could do with another group of peers who were finding their adolescent identity. The band director created a community of learners among these diverse teens as they became an organized unit. Walter Enloe found a group of like-minded "mavericks" on the streets as he traveled to and from an American school in Japan. He was part of an informal community of learners among these peers that was more significant to his development than his fellow students. George Gagnon encountered the same community of learners in kindergarten, Cub Scouts, and athletic teams coached by a favorite teacher in a rural city on the northern plains. He formed lasting friendships with the group of boys who went through these experiences together. Diane Dunlap moved often as a child and at each new school would seek safety for herself and her siblings by searching for trustworthy adults. She looked for caring people who would offer support and comfort for needy children in an informal community of learners. In each new school, she found or constructed a supportive community for herself or her brothers. The common feature that emerged for all four of us is that each of these communities of learners became a group of people gathered together intentionally for the purpose of supporting each other in the process of learning.

Each of us learned how to add healthy conditions to a community so that we could learn along with others in a safe and supportive way. As we saw the immense value in sharing our individual stories with each other, we began to ask for stepping-stone stories whenever we thought we were in a community of learners. We gathered hundreds of stepping-stone stories and draw on them here to keep this book at a very accessible and personal level. These stories begin each chapter to make a connection between our experiences and the explanations of learning circles for professional development we offer in this book.

The second part of each chapter is a brief explanation of relevant theory. In Chapter 1 we offer our framework for these explanations. This framework describes six diverse strands of theory that we brought from our various backgrounds and intertwined as the basis for our thinking about learning circles: **living organizations, constructivist learning, group process, complex systems, optimal experiences,** and **interdependent networks**. We first offer a summary of these theoretical strands, identifying their perspective, acknowledging key contributors, and demonstrating how they are related to the six essential conditions. Then, we describe how these strands are integrated in learning circles as a theoretical framework for the dynamic interplay between a whole and its parts. In subsequent chapters, we supply just enough additional theory for you to become familiar with our sources and some references for further reading. We cite research where appropriate to guide you to further resources. Our primary goal, however, is to present the theory as a framework for reading the stories and examples that encourage a very direct relationship between stepping-stones and teaching practices in order to give you new ideas and skills to use wherever you learn or teach.

The third part of each chapter consists of examples that illustrate how each condition comes to life in learning circles. To make these descriptions more personal, we use examples from our experiences in K-12 classrooms, teacher professional development events, community groups, and other programs for adults and children. Our goal is to provide you with ideas to use that include adequate background so you will understand how others interpreted the activities. Our experience as teachers spans every grade from kindergarten through graduate school. Each of us has been challenged to bridge the false divide between theory and practice as we strive to understand good teaching and learning in all settings. We are convinced that effective learning, whether in a first-grade classroom or a master's degree program, occurs when certain conditions are in place. We have also seen many examples of practice informing theory; thoughtful teachers in K-12 schools have much to teach university professors about learning, just as creative higher education faculty have something to offer their colleagues in K-12. For too long, the unfortunate polarity of theory "versus" practice has kept us apart. Our examples represent good teaching and learning for all ages from preschool through graduate school. We hope that our examples of successful teaching and learning from across the spectrum of learners are convincing enough to bridge that divide. Teachers can learn from one another as colleagues regardless of whether they teach in preschool, elementary, secondary, or higher education classrooms. We encourage you to adapt our examples for your own students.

We hope this combination of stories, theory, and examples will assist anyone who is interested in improving learning for teachers. You may be a teacher educator, a teacher or district office person with responsibility for professional development, or someone who wants to enhance future learning events for teachers. We know that anyone can use these conditions to improve learning.

CHAPTER PREVIEWS

Chapter 1, "Creating Conditions," offers a definition of learning circles, provides an overview of the six essential conditions we recognize in healthy communities of learners, and introduces the theoretical foundations we use to establish a base for our thinking.

Chapter 2, "Building Community," reviews the important organizational aspects of group process related to making learning circle teachers feel like part of an active community of learners. This includes rituals such as opening and closing traditions, celebrations for accomplishments, recreation or "re-creation" through collective metaphor, and refreshments for participants.

Chapter 3, "Constructing Knowledge," addresses the self-directed professional development of teachers in learning circles through action research in their classrooms, descriptions of their teaching approaches and learning styles, and child development studies.

Chapter 4, "Supporting Learners," considers the caring aspects of teachers working collaboratively in learning circles who encourage one another, visit each other's classrooms, and discuss together the important work of teaching children.

Chapter 5, "Documenting Reflection," describes the process of keeping journals, analyzing student learning, videotaping teaching sessions for peer review, and summarizing learning circle gatherings.

Chapter 6, "Assessing Expectations," offers approaches to involve learning circles in establishing common expectations for professional development, setting personal baselines and expectations for growth, and creating and maintaining portfolios to demonstrate personal growth and professional change.

Chapter 7, "Changing Cultures," presents ways that teachers can influence the cultures of their schools, districts, or communities by assuming teacher leadership through surveys, committees, meetings, presentations, or conferences that encourage broader consideration of issues emerging in learning circles.

Chapter 8, "Recreating Conditions," offers suggestions for using the six essential conditions to develop larger communities of learners beyond the framework of learning circles. This would include combining learning circles at a school, community, or district level; moving classrooms toward becoming healthy communities of learners rather than collections of students; and organizing learning communities to address guidelines for professional development and to accept the five propositions of the National Board for Professional Teaching Standards as reasonable criteria.

WHO SHOULD READ THIS BOOK?

This book is primarily for teachers in elementary or secondary schools and those who work with teacher professional development. It is also appropriate for educational administrators, teacher educators, or parents who are interested in effective continuing learning by teachers throughout their careers and by those who are involved in educational or organizational change at any level. At its most profound level, we believe that the processes, activities, and exercises we describe in this book can be applied fruitfully wherever any group gathers to learn together. We propose a departure from the standard agendas for "staff development" and advocate a professional development approach that *begins* with teachers who are interested in learning together about their craft with a supportive group of colleagues.

The time when all teachers are members of learning communities may still lie ahead of us. We believe our experiences with the creation of such communities moves us from wishing it were so to convincing others that it can be done. Whether the leadership comes from teachers themselves, school district administrators, or university-based educators, the goal to create learning circles and communities of learners must remain central to our thinking about professional development. Listen to the words of the many teachers cited in this text, and it will be clear that teachers are in the best position to create the conditions to ensure their own success.

ACKNOWLEDGMENTS

We want to recognize and to express our thanks to all of those teachers we learn from:

> The teacher and professor teams of leaders and our colleagues/ students/teachers in learning communities who helped us pull the six essential conditions out of thousands of hours and experiences. Their voices are heard throughout this book.

> The communities of learners who became the stepping-stones in our lives as teachers.

> The gifted teacher educators who taught us so much by their teaching and who support us in our writing: Pat and Dick Schmuck, Phil Runkel, Linda Lambert, Vito Perrone, P. J. Ford-Slack, Joanne Cooper, Sandy Gehrig, Kay Insley, and Kay Peters.

> The teacher leaders Paul Bianchi, Barbara Dunbar, and Robert Falk at the Paideia School and the genetic epistemologist Jean Piaget.

> Our families and friends, who tolerated never-ending conversations about learning and teaching.

> Our children, who always show us that we don't know everything about teaching or learning.

Baby George Yvon, who waited to be born until the rough draft of this manuscript was ready.

And Alice Foster, who encouraged us to translate our experiences with communities of learners into conditions for teacher professional development.

About the Authors

Michelle Collay is Director of Graduate Education Programs at Hamline University in St. Paul, Minnesota. A former music teacher, she is a teacher-scholar who seeks to improve teaching and scholarship in higher education and K-12 schools through collaborations with educators in and beyond these institutions.

Diane Dunlap is a budding novelist, following her 1997 retirement as Dean and Professor of Education at Hamline University. She is coauthor of many articles, chapters, and books on women in education, adult learning, and professional development.

Walter Enloe is a teacher in the Graduate School of Education at Hamline University. A student of the constructivist epistemology and organicism of Jean Piaget, he taught kindergarten and high school in Atlanta, Georgia, and was the teaching principal of the International School in Hiroshima, Japan.

George W. Gagnon Jr. is an education consultant and math models designer who has been involved in education for 25 years as a classroom teacher, school administrator, university professor, and community learning consultant. His interests include constructivist learning design, communities of learners, appropriate assessment, professional development, and integrating technology.

CHAPTER ONE

CREATING CONDITIONS

*Tenacious habits of mind and deed make the achievement
of strong collegial relations a remarkable accomplishment: not the rule, but the rare, often fragile exception.*

Judith Warren Little
(1990, pp. 166-167)

By the time adults graduate from college and are preparing for a teaching career, they have experienced many formal learning situations. Some are memorable in positive ways, and others are re-membered for negative reasons. But most of them blur together as similar, slightly boring, required events. Many teachers remember more meaningful learning experiences such as work on school news-papers or yearbooks, debate teams, theater groups, bands, choirs, language clubs, 4-H clubs, scout troops, team sports, and other ex-tracurricular activities. These were often their first encounters with learning that they chose, where they could take responsibility for themselves, and where they set their own agenda. These charac-teristics can be found in a high-quality professional development framework. George tells a story about designing such a framework as principal of an alternative public open school in the foothills of Colorado:

> When I arrived as coprincipal, the teachers were working in self-contained classrooms with students at one or two grade levels. Over the course of 2 years, we talked with one another, with par-ents, and with other educators about reorganizing our work and responsibilities. Eventually, we regrouped into teaching teams

1

appropriate for different developmental levels: a Preschool for 3- to 5-year-olds, an Early Learning Center for 5- to 8-year-olds, an Intermediate Area for 8- to 12-year-olds, and a Middle School for 12- to 15-year-olds. There was overlap between these age levels, and students moved freely between them until they were ready to stay with the older group. The teaching teams usually included two teachers and two lay assistants who were responsible for about 50 children. Special teachers and project teachers often joined them for team meetings. These teams organized their own curriculum, communication with parents, and involvement of other teachers; they regulated their own staffing, spending, and schedules; and they adapted programs and processes when their assessment showed it was necessary. These teaching teams were constantly learning and changing as they took responsibility for their own professional development and quickly incorporated what they learned into their classroom practice. Afternoons often ended with members of each teaching team talking through what they had observed and learned about their individual children during that day. Parents were so supportive of these conversations that they agreed to arrange apprenticeships for all students on Wednesday afternoon each week so that teaching teams could have more time to consider individual children and their learning.

These teaching teams were prototype learning circles where a purposeful focus on professional development and classroom planning led directly to a deeper understanding of children and how they learned.

WHAT ARE LEARNING CIRCLES?

Learning circles are small communities of learners among teachers and others who come together intentionally for the purpose of supporting each other in the process of learning. Learning circles can be made up of groups of teachers, students, parents, community members, administrators, or other professionals and can be a combination of members from any or all of these groups. In this book, we focus on learning circles that are typically made up of teachers or other educators who are engaged in their own professional development.

These learning circles might be smaller groups within a larger community of learners but usually are a distinct group of teachers who are gathered together to support each other's learning. Such learning circles can be short-term or long-lived, but they must become healthy communities of learners to differentiate themselves from externally driven district workshops, in-service sessions, or reform efforts. Teachers have choice, can take responsibility for their own development as professionals, and set their own agenda for studying learning and changing their teaching. Teachers who team together at a grade level or in multilevel clusters could already be in learning circles. The power of members of small groups to support one another as learners is an intrinsic part of our social and organizational fabric. Generally, such groups are informal and based on work, friendships, or neighborhood relationships among people who do similar things, have similar interests, or interact with each other on a regular basis during the course of their lives. Learning circles have a variety of configurations and interact with the broader environment of the communities in which members live, work, and play.

The Communities of Learners Schematic in Figure 1.1 illustrates the relationship between learning circles, generic communities of learners, and formal learning communities.

BACKGROUND OF OUR THINKING

We believe that learning is a process of change. We define learning as a process of changing what you know by constructing patterns of action to solve problems of meaning. As humans develop, we experience all four dimensions of our environment: matter, energy, space, and time. We learn to construct different patterns of action in each of these dimensions: physical, symbolic, social and theoretical patterns, respectively. We solve problems of meaning by coordinating movements, establishing routines, inventing realities, answering questions, making decisions, setting expectations, creating metaphors, and building theories.

The four of us came to know each other first as teachers whose practice we respected. Michelle was a music teacher who was told by other students to be sure and take Diane's classes, regardless of what she taught. Diane, a policy administration professor with little training in teaching, began to rely on Michelle and fellow teachers for

Communities of Learners Schematic

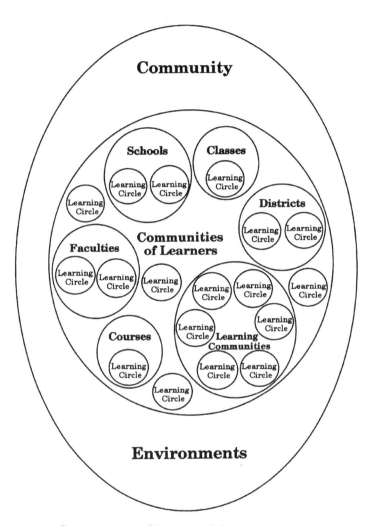

Figure 1.1. Communities of Learners Schematic

coaching her on the teaching process. George was a principal with a love of teaching and a commitment to teacher development. He met Michelle when she was directing a grant to retain rural first-year teachers. Walter was a kindergarten teacher who found adult teaching just as exciting and met the rest of us when we worked together on a program for teacher professional development.

Only when we started talking about our beliefs in better ways to teach did we discover the very different theoretical perspectives in our backgrounds. Three of us began to work in teacher education after several years teaching and administering in K-12 schools. Michelle brought a small group process perspective from Oregon; George brought a constructivist learning perspective from North Dakota; Walter brought a living organization and complex systems perspective from Georgia and Japan. Diane brought perspectives on optimal experience (flow in the zone) and interdependent networks (ecosystems) from her educational leadership work across the Northwest and Canada.

Throughout 2 years of weekly meetings, we regularly revisited the six strands of theory that formed our collective background:

1. Living organizations
2. Constructivist learning
3. Group process
4. Complex systems
5. Optimal experience
6. Interdependent networks

These six strands are now the shared theoretical foundation for our thinking about learning and professional development. The strands represent biological, epistemological, sociological, anthropological, psychological, and ecological perspectives on learning and personal development.

The six strands of theory formed the warp for us to weave the tapestry of our thinking about learning circles. The woof was our own experiences with teaching and learning in community. In this chapter, we give a brief overview of theory so that you will know the foundation thinkers if you wish to understand more about the important ideas that underlie the six essential conditions we describe in this book. We want this book to be a guide to practice, however, and provide only enough warp threads so that the pattern of the woven tapestry can begin to emerge. We plan to provide this theoretical foundation in two ways, first, through the overview in this chapter; and, second, by a slightly more detailed reference to the respective strand in our discussion of each condition. We have tried to write the book so you can begin anywhere in it and refer to the theory

Table 1.1 Theoretical Overview

Theory Strand	Major Theorists	Essential Condition
Living Organizations	Jean Piaget Aril DeGeus	Building Community
Constructivist Learning	Lev Vygotsky Ernst von Glasersfeld	Constructing Knowledge
Group Process	Pat & Dick Schmuck Phil Runkel	Supporting Learners
Complex Systems	Ludwig von Bertalanffy Charles Perrow	Documenting Reflection
Optimal Experience	Mihaly Csikszentmihalyi David Bohm	Assessing Expectations
Interdependent Networks	Robert Kegan Fritjof Capra	Changing Cultures

in this chapter when you are ready. Please don't be put off by this theoretical thinking if you are starting to read through the book from beginning to end. The theory presented here may not be as clear as the practical ideas in subsequent chapters.

Actually, all six strands of theory apply to each of the six essential conditions as well as to the synergistic effects of all six together. Our book would be very long if we described all the theoretical connections we have identified, and the applications might get lost among the citations. Instead, we wanted this book to be a practical guide to improving learning practices regardless of how and what theory applies. Table 1.1 summarizes the six strands of theory, the major contributors to our thinking, and the essential condition we relate to each theory.

We have selected only two representative theorists for each strand in our collection of thinkers. Piaget (1967) offered a biological perspective on individual development as he described the characteristics of a living organization as a self-organizing, self-regulating, adaptive system. Piaget (1974) also described children's construction of reality and how "to understand is to invent." DeGeus's (1997) book on the life span of a "living company" builds directly on Piaget's work as it extends to organizations as well as individuals. Vygotsky (1987) was a Russian psychologist who made us aware of the importance of social interaction and communication in cognitive development. Von Glasersfeld (1987) is a "radical constructivist" who advocated that all knowledge is constructed by the individual learner and not just transmitted by a teacher. Schmuck and Schmuck (1997) and Schmuck and Runkel (1994) brought the work on group process in organization development into schools and offered a framework for conducting school improvement efforts with sensitivity to the interactions between individuals, small groups, and school staffs. Von Bertalanffy (1973) was an early-20th-century thinker who was among the first to articulate the notion of systems functioning as a synergistic whole rather than a collection of isolated individual parts. Perrow (1984) linked complex systems with chaos theory to describe the phenomenon of "normal accidents." Csikszentmihalyi (1990), or "Professor Mickey" as his students call him, described optimal experience and elaborated the concept of "flow" that grows out of personal meaning making and purposeful action. Kegan (1982) characterized "holding environments" where individuals develop interdependently. Capra (1996) wrote about the "web of life" as a network of interdependent systems.

Because of our individual experiences and collaborative thinking, we offer an organic perspective on learning circles that integrates these six strands of theory and our dozen thinkers. We deliberately chose living organizations with their biological functions as an analogy for the development of human living organizations that we refer to as learning circles. These human living organizations also have psychological, sociological, and anthropological processes, because they are made up of individuals who relate in groups and are part of larger cultures. This analogy places the human living organization of a learning circle within the complex ecological systems of schools, districts, communities, and universities where members teach, work, live, and study. It also includes the epistemological processes of knowing as individual members learn within the human living organization. We choose to focus on learning circles as the place where whole communities of learners are in dynamic interaction with their parts or individual members of these communities. Communities of learners can change only as individual members learn. Individual members learn most effectively as part of small groups who support change.

Our learning circles are living organizations that use the theories of constructivist learning and the principles of group process to describe the complex systems of education and to encourage optimal experiences in learning for members. These members also affect the interdependent networks where they teach and live. We focus on one of our six strands of theory in each chapter. Each strand is a foundation for the following six essential conditions.

The Six Essential Conditions

From our studies of learning theory, the learning experiences we shared with each other, and the work of the learning community membership, we identified six conditions common to healthy communities of learners. These six conditions are necessary for initiating, maintaining, sustaining, and completing communities of learners. Taken individually or in groups of two or three, these conditions do not guarantee the formation or health of communities of learners. Each condition is necessary but not sufficient. Taken together, however, these conditions serve as a framework for constructing and continuing healthy communities of learners. Because we see learning circles as healthy communities of learners, these conditions are necessary for the authentic professional development of teachers. These six essential conditions are:

- Building community
- Constructing knowledge
- Supporting learners
- Documenting reflection
- Assessing expectations
- Changing cultures

These six essential conditions for healthy communities of learners were first articulated collaboratively by a group of facilitators who led the first learning communities. This group included Walter,

Michelle, and George. We described our common expectations for the learning events we were about to lead. These were expectations we had for ourselves, for teachers in our programs, and for students in their classrooms. Through our experiences leading learning events for teachers, we found such expectations were necessary for the success of our professional development programs. These expectations became the six essential conditions for creating healthy communities of learners.

We realized that these six conditions not only were useful to ourselves, our teachers, and their students but could be useful for any group of people gathered for the purpose of learning together. These conditions are particularly important for groups of teachers who are taking responsibility for their own professional development, not only because they can provide a ready framework for effective learning but also because personal experience with the framework can be transferred directly into the teacher's classroom.

BUILDING COMMUNITY

The first condition essential for healthy communities of learners is to establish the difference between their community of learners and, for example, courses or classes. Not all learning events reflect efforts to build a sense of shared community during the event. Briefly, building community means making sure members get to know one another, their work histories, their life stories, and their areas of interest. Community rituals can be repeated during most gatherings of the learning circle, such as opening and closing ceremonies, bringing snacks and beverages for the group, treating all individual members with respect, and agreeing to core values that describe ways of relating to others as a community of learners. Such community-building activities promote the feeling of belonging to your own learning circle and of being responsible to the group for your own professional development planning. Building community is a basic condition necessary for empowered learning by each individual and for the group as a whole. We offer more details in Chapter 2.

CONSTRUCTING KNOWLEDGE

The second condition essential for healthy communities of learners is to understand how individuals construct knowledge by making their own meaning and sharing their understanding with others. This is particularly true for independent adults who may need to experience learning this way to use it with children. It is part of how we define being "professional." Teaching cannot be based on telling learners what we think they should know but must be done by engaging them through active learning experiences so they form their own conclusions about situations presented to them. In a successful learning circle, teachers focus on their own interests and questions rather than simply ingesting information from experts who have "the answer." Learning is deeper and more integrated when the professional teacher/learner goes through a high-quality constructivist process. We give more examples in Chapter 3.

SUPPORTING LEARNERS

The third condition essential for healthy communities of learners is to provide support for individuals in their communities through conversations, encouragement, site visits, support groups, and feedback on ideas or changes. Learning circles often give support to members or to their colleagues in work situations and members also maintain regular contact through phone calls, e-mail, and notes. In a learning circle, professionals identify their own interests and agendas for learning so colleagues in the learning circle can support them through active attention to descriptions of learning and sincere appreciation for learning by others. Although the importance of support may seem obvious, most adult learning events or classrooms for children pay very little attention to it. We provide more specifics in Chapter 4.

DOCUMENTING REFLECTION

The fourth condition essential for healthy communities of learners is for individuals to describe and record their internal reflections on learning in journals, reflection papers, and oral dialogues. These reflections should be shared with others through mutual readings or electronic conferences as confidence and trust begin to develop in the learning circle and other members demonstrate their support and encouragement. This documentation becomes more than a simple record of accomplishment as it is also an additional way to construct new knowledge. Structured reflection requires learners to look back at goals set and met or not met, on serendipitous learning and questions that surprised them, and toward insights that may occur when their new learning shifts part or all of their original beliefs about teaching. We describe more experiences in Chapter 5.

ASSESSING EXPECTATIONS

The fifth condition essential for healthy communities of learners is to determine collective expectations and to agree on a process for assessing individual progress, primarily through some demonstration of movement toward accomplishing each expectation. Most of our professional development programs used some variation of the five propositions from the NBPTS (1991). Many learning circles describe baselines for each expectation and then demonstrate individual growth toward meeting that expectation rather than accomplishment of a particular standard. Often, these demonstrations take the form of professional portfolios or video- and audiotapes that capture teachers in action. The difference between determining progress toward shared goals rather than threatening consequences if imposed standards are not met is critical to effective professional development. We elaborate on approaches in Chapter 6.

CHANGING CULTURES

The sixth condition essential for healthy communities of learners is for members to engage in thinking about how the culture of their classrooms and students or their businesses, churches, or organizations could be changed by their individual or collective efforts. Cultures of groups are always evolving as members come and go or as individuals learn and change. Our challenge is to understand how change takes place in different cultures and what individuals can do to influence change. Cultures are always changing, and this realization allows us to acknowledge such change for ourselves, to make change visible to others, and to interact together about how to affect change. Learning circles emphasize the importance of personal transformation and value the impact that a learner can have on another person. Our basic assumption is that change takes place by one teacher at a time transforming what each thinks, does, and says. We explain more strategies in Chapter 7.

The development of living organizations among humans is a lifelong process of *organizing, regulating,* and *adapting* while interacting with all four dimensions of our human environment—physical, symbolic, social, and theoretical. These three processes are common to all living organizations and apply to communities of learners such as learning circles as well as to individual learners. The six conditions we describe are related to the three common processes of living organizations. Building community and constructing knowledge are organizing conditions. Supporting learners and documenting reflection are regulating conditions. Assessing expectations and changing cultures are adapting conditions. We believe that learning circles and other communities of learners are healthy living organizations when they include these six conditions, because they accomplish the constant functions of organizing themselves, regulating themselves, and adapting to their human environment in all its dimensions. We describe how these parts integrate into a whole in Chapter 8.

FOR FURTHER READING

Dewey, J. (1916). *Democracy and education.* New York: Free Press.
Deming, W. (1986). *Out of the crisis.* Cambridge: MIT Press.

CHAPTER TWO

BUILDING COMMUNITY

Education can never merely be for the sake of individual self-enhancement. It pulls us into a common world or it fails altogether.

Robert N. Bellah, Richard Madsen,
William M. Sullivan, Ann Swidler,
and Steven M. Tipton
(1991, p. 176)

Our writing of this book began with the development of a learning circle—our writing team. The four of us had worked together for several years, yet we knew little about the various learning paths each of us had walked. We agreed to start each working session with stepping-stone stories about positive experiences with learning in previous lives. We brought our prior knowledge to the group, gave specific examples about our experiences working in small groups, created language with shared meaning, and connected our theories. Walter related an experience from graduate school when he first saw himself as a teacher:

> My first year at the Graduate Institute of Liberal Arts at Emory University, a group of us received an NEH grant to create a nine-program television series for the local PBS and CBS affiliates on "A World of Choice." We filmed segments at several alternative schools, including the Paideia School, an "open school" nearby. Paideia was led by a critical mass of teachers from Harvard and my college, Eckerd, who had studied the progressive school traditions of England and New England. Paideia was the most compelling.

When I became a teacher over the next 8 years, I really understood how Paideia exemplified a community of learners. Paul Bianchi, the headmaster, saw himself foremost as a teacher even though he was the school's coordinator and manager and a leader of people. We followed him with great admiration and respect because he was one of us and we one of him. We teachers saw ourselves as collaborators and colleagues of each other.

Walter's remarkable experience as a young teacher remains a marker along his road to becoming a constructivist learner and teacher. In retrospect, it is clear that this community of learners contained a learning circle for adults, a place where members were encouraged to be colleagues, where young, inexperienced teachers were respected as contributors, and where each contribution was valued.

These lessons became part of Walter's worldview about teaching and learning, about the relationship of children and adults, and about his role as teacher. The lessons were transformed into his kindergarten classroom. As he moved into the role of learning community facilitator, he asked, "Is community something that needs to be built or does community happen wherever people gather for some purpose?" His query became a guiding question for our learning circle of four coauthors. We revisited our own assumptions about what it meant to be "in community." We had assumed membership in community because we were professionals gathered for a common cause and had observed this assumption in our colleagues. By merely being together in a school, teachers might assume that community is a given. People in community, living or working in a common place, may feel some sense of belonging—shared beliefs, proximity to others, shared customs, traditions, and perhaps reciprocal duties and obligations. Community, however, must be deliberate. We believe that resilient communities are purposefully built or constructed and then continually renewed and sustained. Although many people assume that they will find themselves in a community with predestined common values (e.g., class, committee, grade-level team, school), community is created by each member. It may appear to function, yet without critical steps that must take place for each member and the group, community cannot sustain itself.

WHAT IS COMMUNITY?

Community is often defined by its absence. Most teachers have been members in a variety of communities and enter new ones with tacit beliefs about them. A strategy we use in our examination of community is exploration of our assumptions and beliefs about the profession through the use of metaphor (Lakoff & Johnson, 1980). The use of metaphor through language, symbol, or action can elicit assumptions about what community is or is not and give members ways to articulate understanding. Gareth Morgan (1997) explores how our vision and goals are embedded in the dominant metaphors or language found in the actions that guide an organization. He believes that "all theories of organization and management are based in implicit images or metaphors that lead us to see, understand, and manage organizations in distinct or partial ways" (p. 4). His examples include organization as machine, organization as organism, and organization as culture. For example, if we believe that communities of learners are machines, we might cast learning circles as cogs. If one fails to function, the entire community breaks down. But if we cast learning circles as healthy gardens, then each part contributes to the health of the greater whole in its own way.

We believe that communities of learners and learning circles are organic and growing like human living organizations. Piaget (1974) described intelligence as a process of self-organizing, self-regulating, and adapting to the environment that is carried on by living organizations. DeGeus (1997) echoes this thinking as he describes a "living company" and its habits of survival in a turbulent business environment. We consider learning circles to be human living organizations because they are complex systems interacting with our human environment. We interact not only with our *physical* environment but also with the interdependent networks of our human ecology. These networks of subsystems and ecosystems include *symbolic, social,* and *theoretical* dimensions of our environment. Optimal experience, group process, and constructivist learning represent these dimensions, respectively. Our learning circles are constantly being enriched and modified through interaction with all four dimensions of our human environment: physical, symbolic, social, and theoretical.

Although the machine metaphor is not compatible with our notions of schools, others may have trouble conceiving of schools as a living organization. Nevertheless, schools are made up of living beings in the process of development, growth, and change. Communities form that may be portrayed by a single metaphor, but they also develop and change over time. Peck (1988) speaks of new communities going through a series of phases from "feel good" community to "pseudo-community" to "make or break" community. Professionals initially assume membership because of some common structure or organizational goal, yet as they move beyond the "feel good" stage, conflict arises. When community leadership invites participation, is intentional, and offers clear metaphors about what it believes about the nature of the work, then participants can become members of a culture that is consistent and aligned like a group of gardeners who engage together in maintaining the health of the garden. They create an authentic community based on shared values that lead to mutual respect for others and the reciprocity of rights and responsibilities.

We believe that the core virtues we design for students must be lived by word and deed by their models: facilitators, leaders, and teachers. Senge and Kim (1997) contend that the great fallacy of Western organizational theory is its penchant for "technical rationality," an example being the boss having all the answers or all the power, when in fact the frontline people really know much more about the work. They note,

> If we can let go of this notion of technical rationality, we can then start asking more valuable questions, such as:
> - How does real learning occur?
> - How do new capabilities develop?
> - How do learning communities that interconnect theory and practice, concept and capability come into being?
> - How do they sustain themselves and grow?
> - What forces can destroy them, undermine them, or cause them to wither? (p. 4)

As we plan for professional growth, we focus on living organizations made up of learning circles of teachers seeking supportive settings for individual and group development. In those supportive settings, they can ask the hard questions and create the conditions for learning.

In *The Basic School: A Community of Learners,* Boyer (1995) notes the cornerstones in building an authentic learning community are the culture of values and traditions and the roles that engage the shareholders or partners.

- How do they conceive and describe the culture in which they are embedded physically and socioculturally?
- What are the norms or values and traditions for the ways people treat each other?
- How do the stakeholders conceive their roles, rights, and responsibilities?
- How do they define the nature of the learning community environment in which they live and grow?
- Who leads?
- How and to what degree are the stakeholders making decisions, solving problems, and maintaining themselves and the community?

But community doesn't just happen, even in a small school. To become a true community the institution must be organized around people. . . . What we are really talking about is the *culture* of the school, the vision that is shared, the way people relate to one another. . . . Simply stated, the school becomes a *community for learning* when it is a purposeful place; a communicative place, a just place, a disciplined place, a caring place, and a celebrative place. (Boyer, 1995, pp. 17-18)

The tenets of the basic school offer educators guidance for the development of learning circles, whether they are in communities of learners or stand alone in their organization. The membership of any of these groups, whatever their scale, must be engaged in an intentional and continual process of renewal. The facilitation of this engagement occurs in small, content-focused groups of persons who meet for a specific purpose. In such an intimate setting, members can establish the conditions we describe in this book, building the confidence and certainty required to change the larger organization. Such an organization focuses on its stakeholders working together to solve problems, make decisions, and work purposefully to maintain the well-being of individuals and, ultimately, the well-being of the profession. If the new norms are to be holistic and organic rather than mechanistic, it is especially important that a common language be developed by small groups of professionals making sense of their work. The learning circle is a place for individuals to take back their expertise and make appropriate meaning for themselves, their colleagues, and their students.

We have discussed the importance of individual membership in true community. To sustain itself, the larger community must have a structure in place that is designed by the membership and responds to its needs. We agree with Fullan (1991) that community change or transformation, including the sustaining of communities of learners, requires that five interactive meaning constructs be in place as members examine practices, programs, and organization. The interactions between individuals, learning circles, and the larger learning community are dependent on the following criteria:

1. The quality of shared mission
2. The degree of collegiality
3. The capacity for structural change of time and space
4. The quality of critical assessment, evaluation, and reflection
5. The presence of a critical mass of active, collaborative learners

Communities of learners are dynamic and active, that is, simultaneously ecological and cultural organizations created by growing professionals (D'Andrade, 1992). They are made up of individuals, dyads and triads, and small groups. To understand the relationship of the small group to the whole is to understand learning. We believe that learning is a process of change and presupposes a number of conditions, whether we are learning to achieve and sustain authentic community, learning to transform a learning organization, or supporting human beings.

Communities of learners need a variety of learning circles to meet the interests, needs, and styles of their members. Boyer (1995) suggests that schools transcend the outdated, misplaced debate over graded and nongraded classrooms and establish flexible groupings that meet learners' styles, perspectives, and experiences. Learning circles can include base groups for a sense of home and trust, mixed groups across grade levels or roles, focused groups around interests or for intensive coaching, and governance groups to direct the democratic process.

The stages of development for building community are initiating, maintaining, sustaining, and transforming. We address each of these in turn.

INITIATING COMMUNITY

We have found that creating communities of learners requires first a common purpose or intention to gather together. Individuals come together to initiate, maintain, and sustain a community of learners for all its members. The members acknowledge their interconnectedness, have a sense of commonality and purpose, and respect differences. Within any group are subcommittees or small groups. A community of learners is composed of small groups of persons who form partnerships based on concern for the welfare of self and others and for the common good.

A larger group benefits from the work of the small groups, but large groups cannot function in the same way. Schmuck and Runkel (1994) describe the need to form small groups within a larger group for effective decision making. They recommend that small groups contain four to six members. Examination of values and assumptions about the profession takes place privately in these small groups or learning circles and then publicly in the larger group as individual confidence grows.

The public work of a community of learners is for members to support each other's growth and learning, to share responsibilities for the welfare of the group, and to celebrate individual and collaborative achievements. The shared roles must be negotiated and formulated as the traditions and rituals of the community are constructed. There are rituals for opening and closing the community; decisions are made about everything from meeting times and assessment of the program to expenditures of community funds. Interest groups, grade-level groups, and study groups are created by members. These learning circles, or subcommittees of the larger group, find more immediate success at defining the roles described above. Because the large group cannot immediately function in a democratic fashion, members must have a safe, more intimate place to develop ideas and strategies for working with a larger community.

Learning circles provide the forum for first steps in the development of shared meaning that will extend to the larger community.

One of the first critical processes to initiate community is the development of a covenant. The fashioning of such a covenant takes place in small groups first, then the key ideas are shared with the larger group. A teacher colleague in one of our learning communities was a member of a small group that developed covenants for its own activities. She found success providing her students the same opportunities. Lavonne tells about the changes in her classroom culture because of that process:

> Prior to this experience, I did not really think about or concentrate on building community in my classroom. I have come away from this program with many wonderful ideas to implement in my classroom, but one of the biggest steps for me was allowing students to make the classroom rules. I have tried to create more community and, in turn, a more positive culture. My students have done more work and problem solving in groups. They have also been given additional opportunities to make decisions on the scheduling of activities and types of activities. I have learned that [shaping an explicit covenant] is a key component in creating a strong and positive classroom culture.

Lavonne's description of setting up a group agreement or covenant may seem simple at first glance—many teachers engage students in developing rules, rituals, or classroom expectations. What sets covenant development apart from a single activity is the teacher's belief in the role of the students as members or citizens, rather than consumers of information.

There are many ways to introduce the concept of a learning covenant. Each member can draft a personal covenant with himself or herself about what learning and social behaviors the individual will try to use and which ones the individual will try not to use. These individual covenants can be discussed in the circle. Or, a member of the circle can suggest that someone in the circle record all the ways in which the circle wants to support learning as examples come up in circle brainstorming discussions.

An excellent way to begin individual or group discussion of possible things to include in a learning covenant is to use the six conditions as guidelines:

- What will build community?
- What will tear it down?
- What will support learning?
- What will get in the way of learning?

Members can pose a support and nonsupport statement for each condition:

- How do you think members should behave toward each other to support individual and group learning?
- What kinds of things should we agree we won't do in the circle or outside the circle?
- How often should we review our learning covenant?
- What is essential to each person's sense of human belonging, support, and growth as a person?

When a list has been developed, the circle can discuss the items and decide if there is consensus on including them in a circle covenant. Examples of supportive behaviors would be making a positive or supportive statement after a member has exhibited new learning, agreeing to do brainstorming without critical remarks, and taking 5 minutes in each meeting to review "What we have learned." This is the beginning of a useful covenant that can provide an explicit checklist for monitoring the cultural learning process of the learning circle.

LEARNING CIRCLES OF CHILDREN

Walter related a story about learning from his childhood:

Mrs. Whiteside's sixth grade in Decatur, Georgia, was literally a circle of learning. We always sat in the sacred circle, our desks arranged around the room. In the center was a communal place for group projects and small group work. Mrs. Whiteside emphasized student rights coupled with student responsibilities. The students made the class rules; she was the guardian of our agreements. She emphasized group projects, and I remember vividly my South American study group about Paraguay and the weeks my friend and I put into studying and writing our report on "Stone Mountain" (the largest piece of exposed granite in the world) based in part on a developer's prospectus for turning it into an amusement park.

Children's learning often takes place in learning circles, yet the power of these circles to build community often remains unarticulated. In a project titled Hands Across Seas (Enloe & Evans, 1996), three schools in Minnesota teamed with three schools in Russia, Japan, and South Africa. The stateside schools linked with each other and with their international partners through service learning, video letters, culture boxes, and exchanges. Learning circles for teachers emerged as they gathered each month to share a meal and discuss the growth of the project, their children, and themselves. Through these traditions and rituals of communication, community is initiated over time and distance.

MAINTAINING COMMUNITY

Maintaining a healthy community of learners requires the same activities needed to maintain a garden. The soil must be assessed and modified, new seedlings tended to, and water and food provided; and the garden must be weeded from time to time. For adult learners, management of tasks and rituals is only part of maintaining a culture with the primary goal of fostering learning and professional development. These elements exist within a far more complex and personal, interactive web of individual growth; specific learning about teaching; and evolving group knowledge about school culture, policy, and reform. Nurturing relationships of individual to small group, and small group or learning circle to large group, is at the heart of maintaining a community of learners. It is in these small groups or learning circles that conversations about the creation of common values and covenants take place. In subgroups defined by common interests or tasks, professionals can make meaning of the existing culture and make plans to maintain or modify it as they see fit.

CREATING PROFESSIONAL DEVELOPMENT ACTIVITIES

A "charter" school hired a principal and lead teachers to work together for 6 months to create programs, organization, and curricula using the basic school as a guide. They created a series of innovative professional development learning events to become acquainted; to build trust and civil working conditions; and to elaborate an inter-disciplinary, thematic curriculum. Although advised they should spend additional, in-depth time agreeing on covenants and learning to solve problems, make decisions, and take care of the well-being of staff, the leadership decided that such agreements and protocols were in place, at least implicitly. Within months, however, it was obvious that basic processes for decision making, well-being, and problem solving were not in place. It became necessary to step back and create a covenant for the new community of learners.

Midyear, the whole staff came to such agreements and established lines of communication and consensual decision-making. The lesson was clear; a community will constitute itself and will establish rituals, traditions, and customs. But if participants are not clear about how they treat each other, get along or belong, have meaningful experiences, and have fun, then they ought to consider being purposeful about creating core values and covenants for their community.

SUSTAINING COMMUNITY

Learning circles, however, have no assigned leader, although they often function within a community that does have a leader. This presents a powerful dilemma as the community evolves. Who leads? Who decides? Who makes the rules? Who evaluates? Who's in charge, anyway? These reactions are predictable from teachers who expect and give clear instructions to follow. To the degree that leaders and "participant followers" or teachers and learners are equitable in terms of rights and responsibilities for the work, governance, and evaluation of the community, it is democratic. To the degree that the power structure between participants and leaders is hierarchical, authoritarian, and we-them, the community is autocratic. For example, traditional staff development and in-service education activities directed by outside experts are often autocratic. They focus on particular parts (changing cogs in a machine) without taking into account the holistic nature of both the organization and the participants. Current notions of "site-based management" and "shared decision making" seduce us with possibilities of democracy, yet often share this mechanistic, authoritarian worldview of governance. Notions of care, nurturance, and participation require different metaphors.

Alfie Kohn (1996) contends that both children and adults need not only engaging life work (e.g., curriculum) but a caring community. We also need authentic opportunities to participate as citizens who govern and make meaningful decisions about our community, learning, and work. Site-based councils organized in a hierarchy will not succeed. The Child Development Project (Lewis, 1995) discovered that elementary school students who reported feeling a sense of community in their classrooms were also apt to exhibit low levels of moral reasoning if they lacked an active role in decision making. In reviewing the current literature, Kohn argues, "More sophisticated, principled ways of thinking about ethical questions went hand in hand with community only in those classrooms where students were involved in choosing how to design that community." He concludes, "Community is not enough. We need autonomy, too. In fact, when both of these features are present, there is another way to describe the arrangement that resulted; it is called 'democracy'" (p. 116).

Goodlad (1984) found that teachers want an authentic sense of efficacy, of being heard, of being invited authentically and honestly for advice and counsel. Heidi, one of our teacher colleagues, reflected on her 2 years in a community of learners:

> The first day I walked into that meeting, I came as a graduate student to earn a degree. Over time, I discovered all of us were active learners. During the summer (10 months later), I realized I had discovered or rediscovered we are all professional teachers who learn and teach together. What an insight to discover I had been well schooled and now I was educating myself in a community of learners!

From previous compacts or covenants, agreements can now be crafted as processes for making decisions, solving problems, and sustaining the well-being of the community. We have seen the importance of having these processes in place to address leadership of the community over time. Members must take responsibility for these processes themselves so leaders are not blamed for poor decisions, expected to solve community problems, or become the sole source for nurturing the health of a community of learners.

CREATING A BASIC SCHOOL

Recently, Walter worked with two staffs that had spent a year creating new schools cosponsored by three school districts as part of a desegregation/integration model. The teachers read Boyer's (1995) *The Basic School* and made some consensual agreements about what a basic school was. But there were no specific compacts made around roles. For example, the relations of administration and staff and relations between certified and noncertified staff in terms of decision making, problem solving, and community well-being were not spelled out. Conflict arose when one of the nontenured staff was dismissed. All of the teaching staff signed a three-page letter appealing the dismissal. Walter was asked to mediate between the whole teaching staff and the two administrators at the invitation of both parties. In discussions with key members, it became obvious that there was no concrete agreement about governance. There were no intentional subcommittees or learning circles to provide a place for individuals to gather in small groups and make sense of their new community.

So Walter called a meeting using the basic tenets of learning circles. Participants were asked to agree to a series of ground rules. No put-downs. Civil discourse. I and we statements, not he, she, you, them. Participants then wrote anonymously on 3-by-5-inch cards, public on one side and private on the other, issues or concerns or insights to be made available to the facilitator. They were asked to pair up and use active listening and I statements to hear each others' stories of the significance of their names, how they came to the school, and why they were here. Several stories were shared with the whole group.

Then participants worked in six teams for an hour, moving around the room in carousel fashion to where butcher paper had been put up on the wall and addressing the following general domains for the school concerns:

- Needs
- Regrets
- Successes
- Issues
- Next steps

Each group spent 9 minutes at each station and, by consensus, put its reflections on the paper (each group had a different colored marker so members could track their responses around the room).

The whole group then moved in complete silence to spend 3 minutes reading responses from each of the record sheets and came back to the circle. This time, without invitation, they pulled their chairs closer together. The facilitator asked for their observations, "ah ha's" that neither questioned nor referred to others' comments. They talked as equals to each other and agreed to work with the conflicts they had identified.

Over the next weeks, a variety of techniques, covenants, and cooperative structures for making decisions, solving problems, and being healthy were built into faculty meetings and committee work. Those covenants and structures became purposeful guiding principles about what the participants believed about learning and working in community and became the standard by which they assessed their work and learning.

Transforming Community

The etymology for "community," "commonality," "communication," "communion," and "commonwealth" leads us to a root metaphor or concept, the notion of "common relations." (from the Latin *communis*, meaning "with mutual duties"). If we want transforming communities, we must first be members who are active creators, explorers, collaborative workers, and democratic citizens. As adults, we must purposefully choose a "holding environment" (Kegan, 1982) in which we are both constrained and held and given opportunities to grow in personal and public responsibility. Whether the context is a school or university classroom, adults are autonomous people and professional people who evolve best in a democratic climate defined by a compact of mutual rights and responsibilities. Governance of the group must deal not only with decision making but with the broader concerns of community problem-solving and general well-being, or "public happiness." Individual teachers must be "held" in an adult community and practice shared leadership and participatory governing before attempting to transform their classrooms into similar democratic societies. Teachers who have experienced membership in communities of learners or learning circles are more able to transform their experiences into new settings—their own classrooms, their school staffs, their districts, and their professional organizations.

From Professional Development Program to Classroom

In this next example, three teachers in a junior high school English department became professionally aligned during the completion of an applied research project. They created a constructivist curriculum for their classrooms and designed appropriate assessment to evaluate it. The project became all-consuming as each of them transformed her teaching practice in response to the study of constructivism. Lynn described the changes in the team's professional relationship:

> We're like a community of learners in and of ourselves. It's really interesting how our relationship has changed and how willing we are to be vulnerable in front of each other with the sole purpose to be better educators. We've gotten over having to be "right."

The following school year, they found themselves less interested in lounge conversation and more compelled to meet and discuss ways to further their use of a constructivist approach in their practice. Cheryl offered this example of their transformation:

> We can't sit down and talk about unrelated topics. That's another piece about constructivism that draws us to it, that reflective piece. I don't know how much written reflection we do, but we constantly negotiate information and talk about our teaching.

They were interviewed by a teacher-colleague who had conducted her doctoral research in their classrooms. Kay learned about their team project and was curious about how their students might describe their experiences in a constructivist classroom (Insley, 1998). As a result, Kay interviewed kids and teachers throughout her year of study. Kay asked the three teachers about how their membership in their adult community of learners had shaped their thinking about teaching. Lynn responded this way:

We went through that whole learning process together, we became emotionally and personally connected to what we were
doing, and we defined the journey as we took it. This became
very important to us. We're still taking that information in and
we learn something every day.

Cheryl added her observations about the parallels in the students'
behavior with their adult experiences:

Because there's quite a bit of group work, we see connections
between students that wouldn't normally happen. We see kids'
conversations that they wouldn't normally have. In that way, it's
very similar to what we're doing. We normally would have
talked about our own children, or something that's upsetting us,
or something happening at school. We still have those conversations, but they just don't last very long. . . . We're right back talking about the ideals of constructivism!

Lynn offered examples of how challenging it was to be change
agents, setting off in new directions from the existing school culture:

There are tensions that exist between trying to reach an ideal and
being in a traditional setting. For example, we must respond to
traditional ideas on discipline and deal with overcrowding
while trying to maintain our ideals in the midst of all that. We
rely pretty heavily on each other in coping with such issues as
the graduation standards.

The group discussed the current state of standardized testing
and assessment in the state, demonstrating clearly the levels of professional conversation the group regularly engaged in and had described earlier. Nina suggested that the current state-mandated assessment process was inconsistent:

Standardized testing and the Profile of Learning are measuring
two very different things. One is teaching to one aspect of learning, and the other is teaching to several aspects of learning. So
what are we talking about?

Cheryl closed with a similar critique of the current trends in assessment:

> Constructivism starts with the students making connections to the content, building the inquiry process, getting at, "What does this mean? Where do you want to go with this, what is your experience with this?" The grad students start with a number two pencil, an article about a garbage man, and how Twinkies are made! There is no prior knowledge established, there's no link to the material, there's no data that says that score measures what that student knows.

This conversation took place at 5 p.m. on a Friday afternoon in May. Three teachers set up their classrooms after school to videotape a constructivist learning design lesson with about 20 students they recruited with an offer of pizza. "Teacher as professional" was clearly stated in their actions as they transformed their learning from a graduate program in a community of learners into their own learning circle. They had also recreated learning circles for students in their classrooms. The students who volunteered their time to model a constructivist lesson for videotaping are the other testament to the quality of learning they experienced with their teachers.

BUILDING COMMUNITY TOGETHER

The four stages of building community are initiating, maintaining, sustaining, and transforming. Each stage is dependent on the relationship between individual stakeholders and the social organization as a whole. If we want a whole community defined by the cooperation and just equity and mutual respect of all stakeholders, then the relation between individual (part) and organization (whole) must be reciprocal. Organizations in which the individuals (parts) dominate or overpower the group (whole) or organizations in which the group (whole) dominates the individuals (parts) lead to dominant autocracy; oligarchy; and, in some cases, both anarchy and authoritarianism (Piaget, 1974).

Learning circles act as a bridge between individual members and the total membership of the community throughout each stage. In the small group setting, individuals interpret individual goals, relate stories of personal and professional development, and gain the voice and courage to articulate their contributions to the larger group and to the profession. On return to the learning circles, individuals make meaning of the larger community and the norms, values, and ideals that have emerged from its interactions, and they determine ways to sustain membership within it.

Through our communities, large and small, we find places to nurture and be nurtured as learners, humans, and members of a greater society. Professionals are challenged to create authentic community where it may not exist and to build community with all members present: children, peers, parents, community members, and the greater public. As educational reformers, we will succeed or fail together.

Through our writing of this book our learning circle—our writing team—evolved through tremendous change. Through the telling of our stories with stepping-stone reflections we learned about ourselves and each other, offered support and encouragement during times of personal and professional transitions, and learned to comentor each other as writers. This project "pulled us into a common world" of thinking about our learning, helped us make meaning of our prior knowledge, and gave us a forum in which to develop our language and ideas. We leave the experience richer in ways we could not have predicted.

FOR FURTHER READING

Barth, R. (1990). *Improving schools from within*. San Francisco: Jossey-Bass.

Drucker, P. (1993). *Management: Tasks, responsibilities, practices*. New York: Harper & Row.

Noddings, N. (1992). *The challenge to care in schools*. New York: Teachers College Press.

Powell, W. W., & DiMaggio, P. J. (1991). *The new institutionalism in organizational analysis*. Chicago: University of Chicago Press.

Sergiovanni, T. (1994). *Building community in schools*. San Francisco: Jossey-Bass.

CHAPTER THREE

CONSTRUCTING KNOWLEDGE

*Made aware of ourselves as questioners, as meaning mak-
ers, as persons engaged in constructing and reconstructing realities with those around us, we may communicate
to students the notion that reality is multiple perspectives
and that the construction of it is never complete, that
there is always more.*

Maxine Greene
(1995, pp. 130-131)

Central to the learning circle is its role in providing the time and context for serious and deep thought about ourselves as both learners and teachers. We learn from a variety of perspectives about learning and teaching: from a month-old child and a Japanese sixth grader, from a person with special needs and a person with unusual talents, from the potter and musician whose crafts represent both their teaching and learning, from the teacher of children and the child as teacher, from ourselves learning a new skill such as origami or juggling or dance and then trying to teach it to others. As teachers, we learn from our students by observing and interacting with them in work and play and conversation. Our learning circle might use the same motto as the Western world's first child development study group, the University of Geneva's Jean-Jacques Rousseau Institute, "Learn from the child teacher." As learners, we are constantly con-structing what we know from our thoughts. Our thoughts are feel-ings in our spirit, images in our imagination, and languages in our internal dialogues. As teachers, we interact with others through our conversations, questions, and reflections shared in learning circles to reconstruct what we know. In a learning circle, the participants model ways to share knowledge they have constructed through individual learning and to reconstruct what they know through collaborative learning. In this chapter, we first tell a story about encountering the ideas of Jean Piaget, then describe his influence on our thinking about constructing and reconstructing knowledge, and finally give examples of how this approach can be used in lessons and learning circles.

Each of us came to an understanding of Jean Piaget's work in a different way; Michelle has the most recent story of finding Piaget:

> When I was taking coursework to get my first teaching license, I learned about Piaget in a wonderful textbook called: *A Bear Always Faces the Front.* Henry Dizney was a teacher's teacher who taught Ed Psych from the front of a very deep welled, high-tiered classroom with desks screwed to the floor. He admonished us, "Don't believe everything you read! If you want to know about kids, go down to your local 7-11 [convenience store] and watch them! You'll learn everything you need to know." Obviously, this professor of Ed Psych knew lots about Piaget, but he reinforced my belief that theory wasn't very useful. I didn't think much about Piaget again until George and I started to think together about teacher development. When Diane and Walter joined us to write this book, I accepted my role as the only "non-Piagetian" with mixed feelings. Would I always be the one to say, "What do you mean?" and, "What did Piaget mean?" As a student who experienced much failure in my public school years, I was still quite sensitive about being the dummy in the group. Fortunately, my team encouraged my questions and used them to help us unpack Piaget and others for readers like me—I believed there must be better ways to explain his theory than what most of us had read or heard as students.

KNOWING NATURALLY

Our learning communities and learning circles are built on a series of interconnected assumptions about being and knowing in the world. Our notions of community being a creative, caring, collaborative place are often described by terms such as constructive, constructivist, constructivism, and constructionism. We conceive of our learning as the construction of personal meaning and of teaching as the reconstruction of shared meaning or common understanding. To understand is to invent (Piaget, 1974). Von Glasersfeld (1987) built on Piaget's ideas and described himself as a "radical constructivist" who says there is no way of knowing reality independent of the knower. To know is to construct and to reconstruct. To paraphrase Goodman (1978), reality is not found "out there" independently of us; it is created or constructed within and among us. Lev Vygotsky (1987) was a Russian developmental psychologist who first articulated the idea that knowledge is not just constructed individually but is also a social construction influenced by human relationships, language, and culture. This perspective on being in and knowing the ecophysical and sociocultural environments, including our internal "world," is our guiding hypothesis for meaning making and explanation.

The development of individual humans reflects the evolution of the universe. Each of us is made up of whole and parts. We can construct an understanding of the outer edges of our universe or the inner particles of an atom. We can alter genetic material to constitute new life forms or construct semiotic forms, whether a novel or musical score, that can be reconstituted and valued by others. Human beings are capable of sophisticated imitation that allows us to model the actions of others and self. We intentionally enculturate our offspring through both natural and contrived learning or educational contexts (Bruner, 1996). To paraphrase Piaget's (1967) *Biology and Knowledge,* we are essentially inventors and experimenters who spend much of our time understanding what we have created individually and recreated collectively; similarly, in authentic learning settings such as learning circles we are both learner and teacher, constructor and reconstructor.

Another way to think about how we know is to understand that Piaget's foremost question was, "What is the relationship between 'mind' and biological organization?" This inevitably led him to the question of intelligence and its origins. According to Piaget, "Intelligence is an adaptation" (Piaget, 1936/1952, p. 4). He describes biological organizations as "living organizations" with three constant functions of organization, regulation, and adaptation. The evolution of living organizations is a continuous creation of increasingly complex mental structures and a progressive balancing of these organized structures with the environment. Intelligence is an adaptation of living organizations whose function is to organize the world as the organism structures its immediate environment. Intelligence, then, is not a thing; it is an organizing activity and a process of adaptation that extends our living organization at birth through the ongoing construction of new structures for classification, order, and correspondence.

RELATING WHOLE AND PARTS

The relationship between a whole and its parts of being and knowing has been explained several ways. The original explanation was that the parts dominated the whole, so that objects in the environment were more important than an organism. The revised explanation was that the whole dominated its parts, so that an organism was more important than the objects in the environment. Piaget's insight was that neither the whole nor the parts were dominant, so that a knowing organism cannot be explained without its reciprocal relationship with objects in its environment. This interactive or relational holism is Piaget's main hypothesis about the nature of being in the world and knowing such being. A living organization is a whole open system made up of interdependent parts that operates to conserve its structure by regulation of a balance between its organization and adaptation. Such living organizations interact with the world through an equilibration of external energy assimilation from the environment and internal structure accommodation to the demands of the environment. Human intelligence simultaneously acts physically and mentally, individually and collectively through the constant functions of self-organizing (assimilation), self-regulating (equilibration), and adapting (accommodation), which are in fact largely undifferentiated. In other words, processes cannot be separated totally from content because processes organize content, content adapts processes, and intelligence regulates a balance between the two.

Learning circles are places that own you and you own; unlike space, which is something you move through, a learning circle is a self-constructing place built on a mutual spirit of collaboration and democratic principles of autonomy and choice. Its context and boundaries are the social compacts determined and sustained by its members. Whether in the governing or maintaining of a learning circle or in its actual learning activities, substantive content is process; how we experience a phenomenon is part of what we learn of it.

The following examples illustrate constructivist approaches to learning. They contain "content," but within frameworks created to ensure effective and engaged learning.

DESIGNING LEARNING

One of the basic principles we employ in organizing learning activities for members of learning communities is a process of *constructivist learning design* that George and Michelle developed (Gagnon & Collay, 1996). This process of organizing for learning rather than planning for teaching involves thinking through each of six elements:

1. Situation (you arrange for the students to explain)
2. Groupings (of students and materials)
3. Bridge (between what students already know and what they might learn)
4. Questions (you will ask or anticipate students will ask)
5. Exhibit (of student explanations for others to understand)
6. Reflections (by students on their process of explanation)

These elements are designed to provoke teacher planning and reflection about the process of student learning. The focus is on what the students will do rather than on what the teacher will say or tell them. We no longer refer to objectives, outcomes, or results, as we expect that teachers must respond to the district curriculum or the textbook they are using in their classroom, and they need to think more about accomplishing it than writing it again. We do ask teachers to think through their purpose for the learning they are designing so it is consistent with the objectives, outcomes, or results they are expected to accomplish.

We developed this constructivist learning design together as we reflected on our own teaching with children and preservice education students in university classrooms. The ways we thought about organizing for learning seemed to be just as effective in elementary and secondary classrooms as they were with adult education. The example we offer here is one learning design we constructed together to model this process for teachers in learning communities. We used a set of multibase, manipulative models that George designed called Rainbow Blocks. These blocks model bases 2 through 7. Our purpose was threefold. First, we were trying to introduce teachers to our process of designing for learning. Second, we wanted teachers to experience what it is like for first graders to come to school and have a little knowledge about numbers and then be expected to learn base 10 place value. It seems so easy to us as adults that we forget the struggle we went through as children to master this system. Third, we wanted to give teachers the experience of learning with manipulative models to show them the value of engaging with physical and sensory learning as well as communicative learning. Here is the constructivist learning design that we use for teaching a lesson on bases:

Constructivist Learning Design

Title: Base Blocks Lesson

Teachers: George Gagnon and Michelle Collay

Situation: Teachers will work with models of a base from 2 to 7 and use them to show how they would solve basic problems requiring addition, subtraction, multiplication, and division. Each group will be asked to represent a model of the problem, a solution, and the relationship between them.

Groupings:

A. Teachers will be put in six groups by counting off from one to how many there are in the class. Then, they divide their number by 6 and get into groups by remainders: 0, 1, 2, 3, 4, and 5.

B. Groups will work with the base block models that are two more than their remainder; remainder zero group will work with base 2, remainder one with base 3, and so on.

Bridge: Teachers will each be given a sheet with numbers from 0 to 100 and asked to work in their groups and count in their base by writing each of these numbers. After each group completes its count, it will have to get all of the pieces that model places in their base from a large pile of base blocks.

Questions:

- What do we do when we fill up the first place in base 10?
- What digits do we use in base 10?
- What digits can you use in your base?
- What do we do when we fill up the first and second places in base ten?
- Latisha goes to the convenience store and buys a can of pop for 49 cents and a candy bar for 34 cents. How much does she spend?
- Latisha gives the clerk a dollar bill to pay for her purchase. How much change does she receive?
- Latisha goes outside, and her brother Jamie asks if he can have her can when she is done. He puts it with 11 other cans he and his friends have collected. They will get 8 cents per can from the recycler. How much money will they receive?
- Jamie has to split this money equally with his three friends who helped him collect the cans. How much money will each get from the recycling?

Exhibit: After each group has had an opportunity to work out how to represent the problem, the group's solution, and the relationship between the two, they will have a "See what we made parade" so that each group can explain its work for the others.

Reflection: Teachers will be asked to write individually on 5-by-8-inch index cards about what they learned and what they were thinking during their work together. Then they will receive a copy of the constructivist learning design with the basic elements outlined. They will review it and try to identify what each of the elements were in the lesson they just experienced. A group discussion will surface their observations and speculations.

Teachers develop the **situation** for students to explain, select a process for **groupings** of materials and students, build a **bridge** between what students already know and what the teacher wants them to learn, anticipate **questions** to ask and answer without giving away an explanation, encourage students to **exhibit** a record of their thinking by sharing it with others, and solicit students' **reflections** about their learning. We like to keep the learning design to one page for simplicity and easy reference. The Third International Math and Science Study (TIMSS, 1997) has videotapes of eighth-grade classrooms in Japan that conduct lessons very much the same way. The teacher reviews some previous learning and then presents the class with a problem. The students think about it individually for a while and then form groups to develop a solution. Each group presents its proposed solution for the rest of the class to consider. Then, the teacher ties the lesson together with a demonstration of the best parts of the proposed solutions. This process sounded very familiar to us, and we were pleased to see that test scores confirmed the positive learning from such teaching.

We have interviewed teachers who are using constructivist learning design principles at primary, intermediate, middle, and high school levels. We are also working with a team of three language arts teachers in middle school who use this process in their teaching. We know it can be applied in most grade levels and subject areas as effectively as in math or science lessons for prospective teachers. The time frame often extends for a week or two when students have more demanding research and thinking to explain a situation. A multimedia presentation on the constructivist learning design is complete for other students of teaching to experience how each element looks in writing and video.

This constructivist learning design incorporates the best principles for learning that we have found in our own teaching and lesson planning. Learners are much more engaged if they have to think through an explanation for a situation themselves rather than just being given explicit instructions by a teacher about what to do and why. Most of us learn better in groups where we can think and talk with others rather than just be isolated and quiet. Learners need to take stock of what they already know about something as a bridge to new learning. Questions seem to be the driving force behind most learning, especially those we ask ourselves or that ask us to think about the answer. Exhibiting what we think for others to validate or to challenge is important in changing what we know. Reflection is the primary tool for self-assessment and for making our thinking visible to others. These same principles apply to interactions between colleagues in learning circles and lead to a process of constructing knowledge together as we think collaboratively and learn professionally.

FOLDING PAPER

Learning to fold paper representations is a powerful experience for understanding both how we construct knowledge and how a particular approach to teaching can aid or detract from learning (Enloe & Evans, 1996). Folding paper illustrates how specific learning is shaped by the learner's development and combination of personalities in any learning circle. Origami, or paper folding, is a learning experience that integrates the three symbolic systems of intelligent knowing. Knowing a phenomenon, whether an object, concept, or skill, involves three dimensions: a physical and emotional dimension we refer to as *feelings,* a sensory dimension we refer to as *images,* and a social or communication dimension we refer to as *languages.* We know objects and events from past experiences, and we coordinate relationships between our actions and our symbolic representations of these actions.

We have used paper folding in a number of professional development contexts to illustrate both the power of learning something new, our varying learning styles, and the pedagogical approaches to such learning. Our strategy is a constructivist learning experience of personal and social inquiry involving continual construction, reflection, and reconstruction. Over a 2-hour learning experience, learners pass through five stages of learning:

1. English directions with 26 separate instructions and illustrations on folding a paper crane, adapted from the Nippon Origami Association, are handed out. These verbal directions are given: "Your task is to learn to fold a paper crane. These same directions are followed by fourth- and fifth-grade students. You are to work silently and alone. Do not look at other people's work. If you have questions, please raise your hand, and we will help you."

Participants work alone for precisely 12 minutes. The facilitator then asks, "How are you doing? Who is frustrated? Who is struggling?

Who finds their learning style at work with this process? Who learns easily from following directions or illustrations?" Our experience with American teachers over the past 8 years is that half of the group will indicate struggle, frustration, or difficulty.

2. Each teacher is given a completed crane as an exemplary model. The facilitator then says, "We will now use a Madeline Hunter Mastery Teaching approach to this learning experience. You work on your crane while I talk you through the process." Both mnemonic devices and critical attributes are highlighted as the facilitator demonstrates in front of the group a step-by-step approach.

   A. The facilitator uses mnemonic devices to "prepare the ground," similar to Montessori's notion of preparing the environment, or paper in this case, by folding the paper in rectangles and triangles to prepare the paper for easier folding.

   B. Participants are then asked if they are familiar with the children's toys, "transformers," that change shapes and become different objects. They are then told that these Japanese toys are derived from Japanese origami in which paper is transformed from one shape to another.

   C. Mnemonic imagery related to birds is used. The facilitator says, "Fold the paper as a triangle and then in half again so that you have two triangles. See the triangles as wings. Open the wings, and can you see the bird's beak. Fold it downward. On the next fold make a kite, which then opens up into a large beak."

   D. Finally, participants are asked to be aware of "Nick's rule." They are told that Nick was a 6-year-old in Minneapolis who, after weeks of observing other children fold, said "I know the rule. Whatever you fold on one side, you fold on the other side." He developed his own algorithm.

After this approach of another 12 minutes or so of working alone while the facilitator explains, usually about 50% of participants have made some progress, but few cranes are completed.

3. Next, a video on folding paper cranes is shown. After one 15-minute viewing, about 70% of participants have completed a crane. Discussion after the video centers on learning through watching and

how students' worlds inside and outside their heads are similar to and different from the participants.

4. Participants are then asked what learning context would best help everyone complete the task: cooperative group jigsawing, collaborative groups, sharing meaning, blending learning styles, or working with a mentor. The facilitator would ask about how their culture would accept each approach: "Which would be provided automatically if needed? Which would be tolerated but not supported? Which would not be allowed, no matter how much it might help in learning how to fold paper?" New paper is handed out, and participants work in groups of three.

5. After about 15 minutes in these triads, the facilitator and each group simultaneously unfold the original crane model step-by-step with participants making drawings and relating them to the original instructions and illustrations. Participants then discuss personal learning, new learning, teaching, and styles of learning, first in their triads and then in the whole group. The facilitator then asks members to reflect on what they have learned about their own learning, about how small and large groups learn and function in our society, and about what they might change about this exercise to complete it more efficiently or with a greater sense of satisfaction. Participants are also asked to decide whether the feelings, images, or language representations of the learning task from different steps were most helpful to them in understanding how to fold the paper into a crane.

A learning circle can become an artisan's workshop and a safe place for the inherent differences in learning styles, degrees of risk taking, opportunities for making mistakes, and thresholds of frustration or satisfaction. In classrooms that become such workshops, students may literally teach adults and peers or mutually share in the learning. A sense of equity in a learning circle derives from all shareholders being active learners. One of us first learned paper folding at the feet of a 5-year-old who now remembers fondly, "I taught my Dad origami, and he took a long time to learn it well." That insight reinforces our belief that students need to see their teachers actively learn, make mistakes, be successful, and be open to learning from others.

PLAYING BABY

A third exercise we have used in our professional development work is "Playing Baby." Most teachers agree their knowledge of child development is inadequate, and this process brings understanding of the stages of development to the surface. The exercise also encourages learners to combine experience, construction, reconstruction, and deconstruction of their knowledge in different sequences. Here are the stages of the exercise.

The learning circle begins by revisiting our first 18 months in the world. Our task is to help each other explore the development of object relations and object permanency over the first 18 months of human life, thereby reconstructing through the child our own construction of self and other. Literally lying on the floor as if we were in our former cribs and playpens, we reconstruct infants simultaneously differentiating a sense of self and other. We organize the world (external) as we organize ourselves (internal). The following sequences are documented in Piaget's *The Origins of Intelligence in Childhood* (1936/1952) and *The Construction of Reality in the Child* (1937/1954).

1. No special behavior related to vanished objects.
2. Follows visible objects but does not search for displaced or vanished object.
3. Beginning of permanence (anticipation of vanished object).
4. Active search for vanished object but without taking into account the sequence of visible displacements.
5. Child takes account of sequential displacement of object.
6. Representation of visible displacements.

In summary, during their first 18 months babies proceed from a sort of initial practical self-awareness to the construction of a universe that includes themselves and others as elements or objects. To understand how we construct knowledge and make meaning in the world, we must create a variety of creative, collaborate learning experiences within which to build, explore, experiment, and investigate, much as a new baby learns about the world.

REINVENTING KINDERGARTEN

This learning experience is based on Norman Brosterman's *Inventing Kindergarten* (1997), in which he describes the gifts and occupations of Froebel. Participants are asked to consider the question, "From where do our tools used in teaching develop?" Specifically, who invented the idea or how did it come about that using manipulative arts and crafts was supportive of learning? What were the precursors and the rationale of their use as found in the progressive education theory of Montessori, Susan Isaacs, Piaget, "The New Education," "Open Education," and prevalent hands-on learning in both the contemporary preschool and elementary classroom? We introduce the worldview of Froebel, his early-19th-century natural philosophy of crystals and the interrelationships of wholes and parts, his pedagogy of hands and mind, and his learning steps from constructed solid to plane to line to point and reconstruction to a whole.

The learning sequence unfolds as follows:

1. Participants are organized into groups of three. Each group has wooden block cubes and the participants are asked to remember a story about learning with blocks from their childhood.

2. Each participant draws a representation of the block and then makes a drawing twice the original size. Participants discuss significant learning using a building block metaphor.

3. Each participant is given directions and paper to make a paper box that when turned over is a cube. Each participant is then given directions and origami paper to construct another "solid" without cutting or gluing. Participants journal and then share stories of themselves as an active creative learner choosing the role of actor, builder, explorer, experimenter, or investigator.

4. Using toothpicks and clay, participants each construct a three-dimensional cubic form.

Concluding reflections might include:

1. Discussion on how learning a new skill or concept is both constructive and reconstructive

2. A journal entry on Piaget's contention that to understand is to
   invent

3. A written explication of Margaret Donaldson's (1996) work on
   modalities of constructing a world from here to there to anywhere and everywhere (i.e., constructed whole, plane, point,
   transcendent)

Further reading for the next session would include Eleanor Duckworth's (1987) *The Having of Wonderful Ideas* with her concept about
the "virtues of not knowing" the answer or solution. This becomes
the foundation for further reflection on where our "teaching" tools
come from, who gave them to us, and why and how they came
about. Often, such reflection leads to uncovering our presupposi-
tions about the relationship between learning and teaching or
learner and teacher. Finally, members of the learning circle reconstruct theories embedded in the educational practice of influential or
interesting educators and then construct a new learning experience
for members of the learning circle. From a foundation of Western
education perspective, for example, the learning circle would explore and reinvent the pedagogy inherent in the work of Pestalozzi,
Montessori, Susan and Nathan Isaacs, Dewey, participants in the
early-20th-century Progressive Education Association in North
America, and Europe's New Education Fellowship.

WAYS OF KNOWING

Using the constructivist learning techniques described above
can contribute individually and collaboratively to your construction
of new understandings. As researchers, you can experiment with
teaching approaches and curriculum as you organize and assess
learning experiences for your students and for yourselves. Build on
Jean Piaget's notion that to understand is to invent. Consider
through active experimentation and journaling in your learning circle the ways of knowing described in this scenario, which para-
phrases Piaget:

A child seated on the ground in her garden is playing with pebbles. She gathered the pebbles together, piled them, sorted them by shape, arranged them in a row by size, and matched round ones with flat ones. She admired their color as she described and named them aloud. Now, to count these pebbles she put them in a row, and she counted them 1, 2, 3, . . . up to 10. Then, she finished counting them and started to count them in the other direction. She began at the other end, and once again she found 10. . . . There were 10 in one direction and 10 in the other direction. So she put them in a circle and counted them again and found 10 once more.

Earlier, we described thoughts as feelings, images, and languages. What questions can we ask about this child's ways of knowing?

1. What are her feelings? Feelings are thoughts that represent body actions on objects. She uses feelings in her physical learning as she constructs patterns from her body actions of handling, moving, and playing with the pebbles.
2. What are her images? Images are thoughts that represent sensory actions on or of objects. She uses images in her sensory learning as she constructs patterns from her sensing actions of touching, seeing, hearing, smelling, and tasting the pebbles.
3. What are her languages? Languages are thoughts that represent communication actions about objects. She uses languages in her social learning as she constructs patterns from her communicating actions of admiring, describing, naming, or counting the pebbles.

Physical learning is interconnected with sensory learning and communicative learning. As she placed pebbles in groups or classes by shape, put them in order by size, and made correspondences between types of pebbles, the child was learning about these pebbles. The constructs of shape, size, order (1st, 2nd, 3rd), and number (1, 2, 3) are not in the pebbles themselves but in the relationships she already knows and is applying to the pebbles. These relationships are learned from other people through cultural constructs like words, numbers, notes, and other semiotic forms. The notion of 10 is not a property of the pebbles; it is a construction in her mind based on her previous physical, sensory, and communicative learning experiences.

How is working in a learning circle contributing to your physical, sensory, and communicative learning, and what patterns do you construct from body, sensing, and communicating experiences? In your learning circle, explore other concepts such as permanent object, causality, space, and time. The works of Duckworth (1987), Flavell (1963), and Furth (1969) are helpful for discovering experimentations to challenge your thinking about teaching.

This analysis and the lessons described in this chapter can serve as exercises to engage your learning circle in explorations of objects in the world and transformation of these objects through their construction or reconstruction. Sometimes, this transformation takes place with the objects themselves and sometimes it occurs in our "thoughts" or symbolic systems of feelings, images, and languages. Understanding how individuals use these different thinking styles in their learning is very central to our approach to supporting learners offered in the next chapter.

FOR FURTHER READING

Brooks, J., & Brooks, M. (1993). *In search of understanding: The case for constructivist classrooms.* Alexandria, VA: Association for Supervision and Curriculum Development.

Fosnot, C. (1996). *Constructivism: Theory, principles and practices.* New York: Teachers College Press.

Perkins, D. (1986). *Knowledge as design.* Hillsdale, NJ: Lawrence Erlbaum.

CHAPTER FOUR

SUPPORTING LEARNERS

If students are to be well-taught, it will not be by virtue of bureaucratic mandate, but by virtue of highly trained, well-supported professionals who can use their knowledge and judgment to make sound decisions appropriate to the unique needs of children.

Linda Darling-Hammond
(1990, p. 32)

L*earning* for adults and children takes place within a rich fabric of social interaction, yet the term often evokes the image of an individual struggling to make sense of something in an isolated setting. Because learning is an individual and social event, the circle of people surrounding each learner is an integral part of learning. In this chapter, we present several examples of the importance of support for learners. High-quality professional development should not be a solo vision quest during which individuals are sent away to make meaning in isolation, but a supportive, interactive exchange that resembles the best of an active kindergarten. Social interaction to support learning occurs among adults, among children, and between adults and children.

New learning about professional interaction often happens in formal education settings. The next two stories depict two of our professional development journeys that involved membership in learning circles. We teach and learn as we were taught and learn new ways of engaging learners through membership in a group of like-minded individuals. In both stories, new members of an academic community found the same teachers of group process and were invited to become facilitators of groups. A wonderful way of thinking about large groups, small groups, and learning is offered by organization development research. Two of us had the opportunity to study and practice group process skills with Pat and Dick Schmuck and Phil Runkel at the University of Oregon. Diane recalled her introduction to Dick and Phil, two soon-to-be mentors who escorted her through early stages of learning to teach:

> When I was a new faculty member, many of the professors really didn't want me in the department. Over half of the graduate students in the department were women, but there were no women faculty members. So the dean sort of forced me on the department. They retaliated by assigning me the course nobody else would teach: Adult Education. My department was made up of people from different core disciplines like sociology, history, psychology, and law. The only thing most of them seemed to agree on was that "education" courses had "lower" status than their disciplines. So the course had no status at all.
>
> Luckily for me, there was a critical mass of professors within this department who respected students and education. Two of them were Dick Schmuck and Phil Runkel. I sought their advice about teaching and course content and read all their books. I sat in their classes and I joined them in their research activities. I learned so much from them. They never ignored where a group was at any given time; while they were each filled to the brim with knowledge, they allowed it to come out only when the process of the group was right; and they never used their superior knowledge to belittle others. I learned to draw the adult learners' content from every discipline and to always keep my students at the center of the course.
>
> This cluster of faculty who liked students didn't realize we were a learning circle as such, probably because we didn't meet together intentionally to extend each other's learning and we never negotiated a covenant. However, we learned to depend on each other in the many committee meetings where our paths crossed each week. We took turns teaching together and writing together in different combinations. I still like to be with any of them when they teach because I always learn so much. Without their support, I might never have been brave enough to let go of

the classic lecture style I thought professors had to do. My adult learning class quickly became a place on campus where graduate students told each other to go to learn how to be a professor. Every term evolved in a unique way, built on the unique combination of students present and my own new ideas. Every time I "taught" the course, it created new opportunities for me to learn through active teaching and learning. The best!

New teachers, whether in K-12 or higher education settings, are dependent on such learning circles for their development. Many first-year teachers report finding a single mentor or a small group of colleagues who informally supported them throughout the first trying months of teaching. Diane's story parallels most new-teacher experiences, in which the newcomers start with liabilities such as unpopular courses, poor entrée into the work setting, and little formal support. Given these common circumstances, the learning circle is crucial for survival.

LEARNING ABOUT GROUP PROCESSES

Michelle found Dick and Phil by way of her statistics learning circle, as she recalled in this excerpt from her stepping-stones journal exercise focused on turning points in her educational journey:

As a new graduate student teaching K-12 music during the day, I found myself needing a study group for statistics. I was terrified I would not pass this course and wondered why I was even in a doctoral program. In a class of 60, a few people who sat near me were chatting about their educational administration courses. When they began to plan study meetings, I screwed up my courage and asked to go along.

Stan Crane invited us to his place, where we met Saturday mornings. Six of us met most Saturdays, ate popcorn sprinkled with chili pepper in honor of Stan's Gilroy, California, tastes, and laughed and cried our way through the year. Stan, PJ, and Fielding mentioned a course they were taking spring quarter called "Concepts in OD." I had no idea what OD was, but I didn't want to lose my team, and, as they were in a different division, I knew it could happen. I signed up.

Most of us can tell a similar story to Diane's and Michelle's, citing groups of people that we credit for our survival or perhaps even our ability to flourish in challenging situations. It was not a coincidence that this statistics study group learning circle evolved into the OD Ducks, another generation of an OD practicum group Schmuck and Runkel created called the OD Cadre. The opportunity to be part of this tradition of professional development offered its members the same goals on a professional level as those described by the Schmucks in their latest edition of *Group Processes in the Classroom* (1997). The Schmucks describe four different phases of classroom group development:

1. Membership
2. Shared influence
3. Pursuit of academic goals
4. Self-renewal

The Schmucks' framework of organization development applied to classroom teachers addresses key aspects of classroom climate. Similar in many ways to our six essential conditions, the framework includes the following characteristics:

> A positive classroom climate is one where the students support one another; where the students share high amounts of potential influence—both with one another and with the teacher; where high levels of attraction exist for the group as a whole and between classmates; where norms are supportive for getting academic work done, as well as for maximizing individual differences; where communication is open and featured by dialogue; where conflict is dealt with openly and constructively; and where the processes of working and developing together as a group are considered relevant in themselves for study. (p. 273)

Like us, the Schmucks also describe the relationship of the adult, schoolwide culture to the classroom culture—one does not exist in isolation from the other. Adults need to be participants in a healthy organization to offer the same quality culture to their students. If that healthy support system does not already exist in their school, they need to create it for themselves.

What elements are central to the effectiveness of learning circles? The participants in the group must share a goal or goals. This common goal is created together and made explicit. If the learning circle is truly a safe place for effective professional development, people must be compelled by need to be there. Members of learning circles must feel like contributors, valued members of the group. Finally, the learning circle must offer all members something they are not able to obtain otherwise: ongoing support for their learning. Learning circles succeed when they are really about individuals learning together in a supportive environment.

LEARNING IN SMALL GROUPS

When we recall our richest and most meaningful learning experiences, we realize they consistently took place in the company of other learners. Learning is not a solitary act that takes place in the quiet of one's own mind but a celebratory community effort. Recall first experiences with other learners—on the playground, bouncing a big rubber ball across a school yard, sharing building blocks with other children. Our learning was not only in the handling of the wood, the choosing of pieces, or the creation of a tower, but in our observations of other learners. Our reflections on our acting on an object, however, are even more important than just doing and watching. Through our descriptions and our storytelling run the threads of our understanding of the material and affective world.

Professionals continue to use dialogue to make meaning of their experiences. Teachers carry powerful images of life in classrooms in our minds and hearts as we formally enter the profession. Many years of participant observation as students in schools have given us a backlog of memories, values, and understandings about what it means to teach. If we are fortunate, our student teaching or intern experience was a time for us to place language and meaning around events, feelings, and new knowledge. Sadly, very few practicing teachers find themselves in professional settings where they can reflect on and describe their learning to another professional.

The learning circle must

1. Build and sustain conditions of trust and safety
2. Build conditions of collegiality that support all learners
3. Sustain an atmosphere of learning that encourages risk taking

First, it is important that individuals feel they can trust the other members of the learning circle to support new learning. We must feel safe enough to take risks in new knowledge or behavior. Building and sustaining conditions of trust and safety not only support the feeling of belonging to a community but also allow learners to experiment in a safe setting.

Second, if others are experimenting with their own learning, freely making "errors" in order to learn, it is easier for us to learn new things. In addition to feeling it is safe to make a "mistake," we feel membership in the company of others who support learning. It is important to know others are cheering us on in our quest for knowledge and will not judge us a "failure" as we experiment with new behavior or techniques. Unfortunately, part of the definition of being "adult" is being someone who is competent and who knows how to get through each day with success. Few of us let the need to be seen as competent drop away so that we can learn a new skill. Learning with others allows each learner to act as guide, supporter, and coach to the others.

Third, it is important to develop and sustain conditions in the learning circle that support and encourage risk taking. We know that support and encouragement are necessary to learning and growth and that the culture of a learning circle must be established and nourished so it can sustain its members. Without careful development, the learning circle will not be a source of sustenance and will limit rather than extend possibilities for learning.

Probably the single most significant finding from our years of working with large and small groups of learners is the importance of small groups for adult development, whether they are stand-alone learning circles or learning circles within a larger community. Here is what Jennifer said about the significance of small groups to her learning:

I have used cooperative grouping practices in the past, but as we used them more and more as adults, I was reassured of the value of this process. Other people's ideas and opinions were honored and valued. I found by working together and pooling our knowledge, we gained many more ideas than if we had been left to our own merits. Varied methods of grouping were used, so I was always in different collegial groups. I now do more grouping [in my classroom] and vary the ways that these groups are formed. By doing this, my second graders get a chance to work with and relate to all members of their community.

The next excerpt focuses on the need for safety and trust. If safety is key to professional development, large group, externally driven professional development activities have little chance for success. Each individual needs a personal link to his or her learning. Jeff saw the link between his personal development and the transformation of the school culture:

Membership in this [learning circle] influenced my personal transformation. This process affirmed that what I have been doing with students these past 10 years was right to do. I needed to know this. . . . I can more confidently argue that enhancement of the whole system through [personal and small group] support depends on using [students] to strengthen school culture.

The importance of using learning circles within larger groups is our most consistent finding in our years of study and practice. As one member describes it, "The purpose of the [learning circle] was to anchor the individual to the larger community by providing support and feedback. . . . Members were motivators and decision makers and a source of a great deal of good advice." We have learned that although larger groups such as school staffs can function as a whole, the notion of "anchoring" is an important one. Only in the safety provided by close colleagues can most of us work through the fears of judgment we carry. Teachers who create learning circles can incorporate the six essential conditions and take charge of their own professional development.

Throughout our careers, each of us found extraordinary groups of people who supported our learning. In the next sections, we describe three groups of adult learners: preservice teachers, experienced teachers, and teacher researchers.

SUPPORTING PRESERVICE TEACHERS

George did not attend college with the intention of becoming a teacher. He relates the story of a community of learners led by Vito Perrone that introduced him to the idea of becoming a teacher:

> The last year of college, I became involved with the New School, an experimental program at the University of North Dakota designed to involve teachers in open education. The dean of this institution was Vito Perrone, who became my mentor, advisor, and model for leadership in education. Decisions were made by a consensus of the group involved. He was very participatory and inclusive, asking all to share their opinions and to agree with a course of action all supported.
>
> Vito's philosophy was that teachers will teach the way they are taught, so we had wonderful professors of poetry, art, religion, and psychology rather than traditional methods instructors. Doctoral students became resources for undergraduates, and classrooms of master's degree interns throughout the state were laboratories for us to visit and to learn about open education. The feeling was one of innovation and change in education, with a focus on the students and their learning rather than on the professors and their teaching. Conversations were about Dewey and Piaget, Holt and Kozol, Postman and Weingartner, Barth and Kohl, and the Silbermans, all of whom were writing about educational reform. Many of them even visited us to talk about teaching. We studied language experience, manipulative math, hands-on science, and social studies simulations. Our studies evolved from what we needed and wanted to learn rather than from a prescribed curriculum. This experience shaped most of my 20 years in education as an elementary teacher, school principal, and university professor.

George's learning was supported by experienced role models who created and offered leadership to young adults. Rather than being told as young teachers how to teach, they were invited to learn in ways they would later engage their children in learning. By offering adults the opportunity to "learn as they might teach," Perrone and his colleagues created a forum for all learners to become members, full participants, and leaders in education. This community functioned in small groups or learning circles within the college, was led by several thoughtful faculty, and focused on a variety of disciplines.

SUPPORTING PROFESSIONAL DEVELOPMENT

The need for individual choice and small group interaction during activities that extend personal and professional development is well documented. Too often, staff development efforts focus on a "one size fits all" in-service model, where district leadership inoculates the entire staff with the same medicine. Forms of staff development that respect individuals are those where teachers choose a workshop, a study group, a degree program, or specialized training for themselves and implement new learning with a colleague group to sustain them.

Teachers conducted reviews of personal growth and professional development in learning circles. In reflecting on that experience, peer support was identified as important for emotional and academic well-being. The following point made by Nancy was echoed by many of her peers:

> The most helpful activities were peer group sharing. My peers are invaluable sources of ideas and information. I feel extremely comfortable having them as a support group, feedback panel, and an evaluation committee.

This teacher reminds us of the importance of colleagueship preceding evaluation. There are few groups of adults who could come together and open themselves to colleague critique without having confidence that peers will offer support and affirmation as well. The next description by Deborah revisits the structural roles provided by a learning circle and adds the importance of personal and professional validation:

> What I need in an advisory group [learning circle] is support. I need to be able to give and receive curriculum ideas. I need constructive criticism and guidance when things are not working out. I need to be able to talk frankly about my feelings, personal or work related, and feel that I am safe and that people are

listening. I need to be validated as an educator as well as be able to validate the others in my group for what they are doing.

The majority of teachers in graduate programs designed for professional development voiced similar needs. This teacher outlines the importance of legitimate professional interaction for growth. Teachers, as isolated decision makers, seek out critical reflections of others and flourish when it is provided in a respectful setting. Affirmation of colleagues is necessary for adult development and personal transformation, especially in a "professional culture" that is still defined as unprofessional or semiprofessional. Teachers live in a society that simultaneously expects them to save the world and condemns them for their lack of success. Personal support and affirmation may be more important than any other factor affecting teacher professional development.

As teachers move from feeling like "hired hands" or nonprofessionals to teacher-scholars and teacher-researchers, learning circles provide the structure and support they need to feel confident and capable. In schools that reflect the industrial age, the prevailing metaphor suggests that teachers are workers on the assembly line, principals are line bosses, and central offices represent management. Central office makes decisions about what kind of inservice is appropriate, calls a large meeting, and puts employees through their paces. For teachers to gain power in such a culture is almost impossible without the support of like-minded colleagues. Learning circles provide a place of safety, encouragement for exploration, a nurturing environment for the research of new ideas, and peer review and critique to reflect new learning.

Learning circles of a few teachers or a department are critical to professional development in schools. Seldom do a majority of people in any profession have the same needs or seek the same conversation. Professionals who share an agenda must take the responsibility to create and sustain a healthy subgroup within the larger culture as they pursue their own work. Often, these learning circles will touch other like groups or grow—but they are necessary for individual change.

In a large suburban high school, five teachers worked with grant support to create a "school within a school." They represented five departments: English, math, science, social studies, and art. Charged to create an engaging, interdisciplinary curriculum for 125 students who were "falling through the cracks," this group formed a learning circle that met over a 2-year period to design and implement a non-traditional, interdisciplinary program. The most impressive learning for the members of the circle was newfound respect for each others' disciplines. The long-standing hierarchy that placed science higher than English and English higher than art crumbled because of the respect each member brought to the effort. The teachers developed conditions of trust and safety, with collegiality to support each member of the group, and sustained an atmosphere of learning and encouraged risk taking. They were clear at the outset that unless they could create such conditions for themselves, they would never be able to transform their own teaching for the benefit of their marginal students.

Much as the peer-coaching literature (Joyce, Weil, & Showers, 1992) espoused, we all need colleagues to model, support, and encourage us as we take risks and move in new directions. Although thoughtful school leaders use subcommittees to forward school- or districtwide agendas, we should not assume that all learning circles will influence larger groups of which they are a part. In the case of this team, they remained outside the mainstream culture of the high school and were continually challenged to regain membership with the staff. As their students were considered "marginal," so this elite team joined the kids on the margin.

SUPPORTING TEACHER RESEARCH

There are many fine examples of teacher-research learning circles. Eleanor Duckworth (1987), in *The Having of Wonderful Ideas*, describes a group of science methods students who were studying the phases of the moon. Sandra Hollingsworth (1994) leads a group of urban teachers in their study of literacy in their classrooms. Jean Clandinin and colleagues (1997) met in Calgary, Alberta, to facilitate a circle of support as they made meaning of their "professional knowledge landscapes." Diane met for 2 years with a group of teachers, counselors, and administrators as the group was building a new method of supervision by building on the professional experiences. Although some groups are organized by university faculty, it is becoming more common to see teacher-guided research efforts, such as a group of four teachers we know who provided paraprofessionals

in their school with the training and materials to carry out more deliberate support of at-risk students. They did not need a "leader"
from outside their team but rather wrote a grant, provided the
leadership for the project, and designed the assessment procedure
themselves.

In other cases, teachers develop expertise in a specific area
through reading, writing, and research, and many of those identify
the importance of that work to their professional self-concept. James
reviewed his journey since completing his research project:

> The completion of my applied research project brought another
> dimension to my studies. I have been asked to write about it for
> several articles, grants, and award applications. I have shared it
> with our community and will be presenting it at a national con-
> ference. It was an enormous commitment of time and energy
> that ended with a feeling of accomplishment.

These teachers offer a professional dimension to their school
staffs, districts, and colleagues statewide through sharing their new
learning. In the past, teachers who conducted school-based research
and became "expert" were not always acknowledged at the school
site, but we have evidence that is changing. Susan talked about her
research topic as "important to me and my school":

> The applied research project was the most valuable to me be-
> cause I was able to concentrate on a topic that was important to
> me and my school. . . . I found the constructivist and assessment
> ideas very valuable to my classroom and the classroom culture
> ideas also were very useful in developing good student-teacher
> relationships.

Successful school reform and related professional development
happens one small group at a time. For example, many teachers
seeking support in their journeys toward more holistic thinking
about literacy and its assessment belong to groups such as Teachers
Applying Whole Language (TAWL). These professional support
groups came about because of the criticism innovative teachers felt
and faced as they conducted their own research and adopted new
approaches to the teaching of literacy. Teachers meet once a month to

study research, share resources, and offer emotional and professional support to colleagues undertaking the same kinds of transformative journeys. The stories we hear from professionals who feel like pariahs in their schools beg the question, How is it that schools continue to stymie the best and the brightest thinkers and their support must often come from without? In any case, persistent teachers do find such support in study groups such as TAWL, as well as in small groups within grade levels or across their buildings.

Three teacher colleagues at an urban junior high school formed a team to develop a peer mentorship program for their students. Two were special education teachers. Renee had a resource room of severely mentally and physically disabled students, Ned had a caseload of mainstreamed students. Tina was a regular math teacher. The need grew out of their response to staffing one student, an emotionally disturbed young woman of 14 in Tina's math class and Ned's special education program, Rayelle. The team decided she would find success by mentoring students from Renee's "severe" group, believing that she needed to be needed. Renee set up the mentoring pair, identifying one of her students who needed physical support to move about the building. Tina excused Rayelle from math class 5 minutes early each day for a trial period so she could escort her physically disabled peer across the building. Ned met with the mentoring students' parents and Rayelle's other teachers to advocate for her to receive "special treatment" and be allowed to mentor her peer throughout the day.

The three teachers met weekly throughout the year, supported each others' efforts to change school norms, and encouraged each other in their regular roles as they became familiar with the work routines of their colleagues. They conducted an evaluation of Rayelle's progress in math class as well as her attendance, her relationships with other teachers, and her behavior contract. They also documented their emergent student mentorship program in a case study and presented it to the district so it could be expanded to other students. Rayelle moved from a quiet, unresponsive young person to an engaged, forward-looking 14-year-old, and her three teachers moved into roles of school leadership.

This team exemplifies what Lambert and her coauthors (Lambert, Dietz, Kent, Collay, & Richert, 1996) call a "constructivist collaboration":

These are the actions and interactions among willing participants that result in learning. Constructivist collaboration usually involves a combination of talking, listening, observing, doing, thinking, and reflecting. Collaboration has a variety of purposes and is often initiated by a specific focus or need. The process of collaboration may lead to discovering emerging understandings, purposes, and needs. (p. 75)

What other needs for collaboration compel teachers to form learning circles? Teachers gather in schools for extrinsic and intrinsic reasons. Several teachers on a school staff who share a common goal might enroll in a workshop, course, or program. If participants need to apply new learning, implement strategies, or conduct research in their classrooms or schools, they might meet to strategize about the work. For example, several teachers in a suburban school are seeking NBPTS certification. They meet together every other week before school to review their progress, share ideas, and support each other through the process of developing their portfolios and meeting the strenuous requirements of the NBPTS (1991). The leaders of that effort structure support meetings for their participants as well, providing professionals undergoing a serious examination of their practice a place to make meaning of their shared experience.

When teachers can be professionals and have the autonomy and personal support necessary to move away from the "normal," or perhaps "institutional," behaviors described earlier, they are able to reconfigure notions of teaching, learning, and leadership. These teacher teams may see themselves as closed learning circles, yet they may have an influence on greater numbers than just their students and each other. As we present the relationships of part to whole throughout our thinking, the interactions between formal and informal learning circles and the greater community in which they reside must continue to be explored. One small group of reformers does not a movement make—but pioneers must be encouraged and nurtured on their journeys.

FOR FURTHER READING

Lieberman, A. (1988). *Building a professional culture in schools.* New York: Teachers College Press.

Schmuck, R. (1997). *Practical action research for change.* Arlington Heights, IL: IRI/Skylight Training and Publishing.
Seldon, P. (1991). *The teaching portfolio.* Bolton, MA: Ankar.

CHAPTER FIVE

DOCUMENTING REFLECTION

In order to broaden and deepen their capacity for reflection-in-action, professional practitioners must discover and restructure the interpersonal theories of action which they bring to their professional lives.

Donald Schon
(1983, p. 353)

Theories of action are discerned only through reflection-in-action, according to Schon. Reflection can be done individually, in small groups, or by a scribe for a large group such as a school staff. Reflecting on one's actions, however, is central to making meaning of work and becoming a professional. George describes the value of documenting reflection in this recollection of his school leadership role:

During the mid-1970s, I was a "coleader" of the principal team at the Evergreen Open Living School. We spent 2 years as a community of teachers and parents working on a reorganization of the school. We met weekly as a faculty, had Parent Advisory Council meetings every 2 weeks, and held retreats with both groups together at least twice a year. The existing organization was self-contained classrooms with individual teachers, and we knew that was not what we wanted. However, what we did want was not quickly emerging with a consensus of all involved. A secretary or self-appointed "scribe" usually kept notes on the discussion, which often seemed disjointed and confrontational. Some parents volunteered to be consultants on organizational development and communication. We learned a lot about stating our mission and conducting group process from them, but progress toward a reorganization was quite slow.

In the spring of the second year, we decided to have individuals and small groups write about their visions of the school. As we struggled to articulate our thinking, a wonderful thing happened! We became clearer about saying what we each wanted, we could compare ideas for similarities and differences, those not able to attend meetings could feel involved and give feedback, and we could all see our progress. Our reflection was finally being documented in a form that let the entire community participate and monitor the process. We valued the collaboration and teamwork so much that we eventually reorganized into four teaching teams focused on appropriate developmental levels with gender balance and combinations of teachers and lay assistants. We also determined that the physical space did not meet our needs very well, so we worked with a parent who designed schools as an architect. We all agreed to put in exterior doors and interior walls and doors so the hallways could be used for group or individual study and to move teaching teams into the most usable rooms. We continued to tinker with places and spaces but retained a value for describing our thinking for others. Many of our written reflections became part of a report on the "conceptual model" of our school for a Colorado State Department of Education grant to fund innovative and exemplary programs.

Those who tout "reflective practice" as the most important aspect of professional development are right. Practice without reflection on it is not practice at all. Schon's (1983) *The Reflective Practitioner: How Professionals Think in Action* and other thoughtful pieces about the reflective practitioner gave us a language to use in our reflections about our own knowledge. Many teachers have told us, "I don't have time to keep a journal." Yet, we know how important reflection is for professionals to make sense of their lives and roles (Cooper & Dunlap, 1991). Again, just as learning is not an isolated act, reflecting is not done only in a journal in the privacy of a room of one's own. Often, reflection takes place as dialogues with colleagues about something that happened during the day: an exchange with a student, the unfolding of a lesson, or thoughts about the profession. Some teachers make a record of these reflections in notes or on tape. Others find time to write these thoughts in a special notebook or diary. Reflection is more than writing down thoughts about the day—reflection is as deep and diverse as the people who do it. In this chapter, we first explain how complex systems theory relates to documenting reflection, and then we share a powerful sequence of activities teachers have used to document reflection.

COMPLEX SYSTEMS

One of the first to describe *systems thinking* early this century was Ludwig von Bertalanffy (1973). His general systems theory has led to more recent study of complex systems. Classrooms and schools are examples of such complex systems, and a characteristic of complex systems is that one person, regardless of his or her location in the system, cannot see or predict every interaction that will occur. Teachers and principals are aware of this practical experience of complex systems on a daily basis. Enough unexplained interactions take place to produce other unwanted and unintended actions. Any teacher who has tried to teach a lesson on the last day of school before a long-awaited holiday knows just how many unplanned interactions can occur that will disrupt a lesson!

Charles Perrow (1984) called these unwanted occurrences the "normal accidents" of everyday complexity. He and others argue that increased communication in an atmosphere of support is the only way to keep the complex system thriving instead of being destroyed by its own predicted complexity. That is why we describe complexity here. Documenting reflection by everyone in the learning circle, on a continuous supportive basis, ensures not only the health of the individual learner but also that of the whole group. One of the ways to understand a complex system is to describe its irregular patterns. Teachers can become aware of these patterns in the complex systems of classrooms and schools by seeing them emerge from their reflection as they revisit what they have documented.

A LETTER TO MYSELF

As teachers begin new chapters in their journeys of professional development, it is critical that they have time and support to set individual goals. This moves professionals toward a self-directed curriculum and away from the inoculation model of most "inservice" activities. One way to reflect on individual hopes is to write ourself a letter about what we hope to accomplish along the way. For each of us must determine our own goals, our hopes and dreams for ourselves as learners and then name what it is we hope to accomplish. So often, our experiences with inservice or staff development are not about us—they are about something outside of us, something disconnected from our reality, something reflecting "the district's" or "the state's" agenda. Ownership of the journey is the first step to personal and professional transformation. Learning is not something one gains "going along for the ride" but a deeply personal series of events that can change our lives and our practice.

These letters should be written early in the experience of membership in a learning circle, in a relatively risk-free and disruption-free environment and in a quiet space. The content may be kept private, but members of the circle are usually excited to share ideas or hopes they have articulated in their letters. The stationery should be lovely, and the papers and envelope should match. The quality of this experience must not be undermined by hurriedness, cheap materials, or thoughtless facilitation. If we can learn to take care of our learning, we have a much greater chance for success. The letters are collected and saved for a ceremonial reopening at the end of this leg of the journey or at the beginning of another.

Karen wrote this letter early in her graduate education experience:

Dear Karen,

You are beginning your second term of the first year of this Master of Arts in Education program. How are you feeling about it? I think that if I were you, I'd be feeling pretty good. You are on a journey to better yourself professionally. It's pretty exciting to be back in college, isn't it? And isn't this program great? It sure beats sitting in a classroom listening to a lecture and taking tests, doesn't it? I think you are going to learn to great deal of worthwhile stuff.

Do you feel pampered? This is something you are doing for yourself! For so long you were busy being a wife, teacher, mother, etc., and now you are a student with someone "taking care" of you! I find it's like so going home to Mom and being a little girl again. How has Ed been? Knowing him, he's probably been super about you being gone all weekend. He probably does all the laundry and takes good care of the kids. You are so lucky to have a great man like him in your life—you know that, don't you?

What will you do when you are done with the program? How will it change your life? One bit of advice, Karen. Promise yourself that when you are done and get that degree, you will do something valuable with your learning. Make your life better in some way. Do something new, take a risk. Don't let your journey end here!

Good luck and lots o' love, your best friend, K.

Karen's letter demonstrates the important place of personal development in professional development. She focuses on her family's development along with her own and sees her foray into formal study as a privilege. Her ability to engage in extended learning is linked directly to the support of her family. In graduate education, we see the need for family support, especially for women students who have families. Karen also placed herself along a continuum of a journey, marking the points of her learning. Reflections on former learning and hopes for the future often find their way into such reflective exercises. Her personal reflections, however, led directly into an examination of professional goals. They are linked.

In the professional development cycle of a school, the academic year is a natural cycle. Teachers might invite each other to meet in topic or interest groups, or perhaps in grade-level groups that meet on a regular basis anyway, and at the beginning of the year, write letters to themselves about their hopes and dreams for the year. Members of small groups or learning circles can share parts of their letters with each other and discuss ways they can support each other in attaining their goals. For instance, if one member hopes to improve his knowledge of literacy, others might suggest books to read, a course to take, or an institute to attend and encourage him to report back to them on return.

As we mentioned earlier, "a letter to myself" is very appropriate for professional transitions. Here is an excerpt from a letter Michelle wrote toward the end of a 2-year professional development experience:

This program was psychic food and water which sustained you during a drought of developmental understanding. Yes, you learned . . . but often, didn't know what you were learning.

Many times, you were impatient with yourself, not acknowledging the change, growth, or perhaps, contributions you made to your community. Remember to look outward at your companions as you travel—not so much inward as you have.

For Michelle, such letters help identify her markers along a path of personal and professional growth. The time it takes to pen a few thoughts is well invested, as such writing elicits beliefs about our relationship to new learning. Those words make explicit the tension most of us feel about new learning—although we relish new experiences like a cool drink in the desert, we may also identify the ground around the learning as barren. Quite a contradiction in thinking!

REFLECTION ON STEPPING-STONES

"Stepping-stones" is a journaling activity Progoff (1992) described in his book *At a Journal Workshop.* In this exercise, journal keepers identify key events that shaped their lives. "The Stepping-stones are the significant points of movement along the road of an individual's life" (p. 76). As a graduate student, Michelle learned a similar method of documenting reflection from her advisor, Rob Proudfoot, who invited first-year teachers to create a road map showing each year in school and noting any memories from that year. He used the reflective process to demonstrate to new professionals the powerful links between their own life experiences and the values and beliefs they held as teachers. She used the same technique for personal/professional reflection to enable new secondary teachers to articulate individual beliefs about the role of teacher.

A group of teachers working to design an interdisciplinary curriculum can conduct this exercise for themselves. As they examine their current curriculum and imagine a new one, they might recall a course, workshop, or learning event that they consider "interdisciplinary." In their learning circle, which could be the curriculum committee or their department, they each tell that story about that learning event. In sharing these stories, members first come to understand their own histories with such a curriculum and how that history shaped their beliefs. They also gain knowledge and empathy about the values held by the others. Documenting such reflections serves the individual and improves the group's chance for success.

Experienced teachers value documenting reflection about their work, especially after many years of practice when their own professional development appears in broader brush strokes. They ask themselves, "Where did my ideas about teaching begin? Do I still value the same kinds of teaching, or do I wish to evolve in new directions?" These next thoughts are from a seasoned teacher completing the stepping-stones exercise. Eve recalled a conversation with her high school guidance counselor about whether she was "college material." His review of her SAT scores indicated she was not.

He assured me that I would not even be considered by most schools because I did not have a "qualifying" score. That brief meeting and conversation created doubts in me that have been difficult to get rid of ever since. I aimed no higher than the local university in my hometown and felt lucky that they accepted me with such marginal SAT scores. Even if I graduated 16th in my class, received awards for citizenship and scholarship, and was given a 4-year scholarship for tuition and books, I was still not really capable. Those test scores said I wasn't bright, wasn't a "Merit Scholar." I've always been waiting for the other shoe to drop, for that test I would fail, for someone to really find out I was a charlatan. These doubts have followed me though a very successful college experience, 25 years of teaching, completion of over 30 graduate-level courses, presenting numerous workshops and courses, and they are still under the surface.

Eve works in an inner-city elementary school with emotionally disturbed kindergarten children. Her profound belief in all children and her dedication to the belief that every child can learn is central to her practice and based heavily in her life history. Eve's story reflects dozens of stories we have heard from capable, experienced professionals. The building blocks of self-esteem, tumbled off their foundation by thoughtless teachers and other educational leaders throughout our careers, can never be reassembled in quite the same way. The scars of unfortunate interactions stay with us for life and must be managed and modified through patient, thorough reflection. The more carefully the reflections are documented, the more progress each of us can make with self-understanding and subsequent practice.

METAPHOR AS REFLECTION

The use of metaphor as a reflection technique has proven to be a wonderful strategy for exploration of our assumptions and beliefs about the role of teacher. From these metaphors emerge powerful descriptions of the tasks and the purpose of teaching. Creating metaphors can be done with written prose, sketches, physical structures designed with tinker toys or blocks. Teachers' beliefs about their roles emerge: Were they gardeners watering tiny seeds so they might grow into strong trees? Or were they guides, leading troops of scouts across a raging stream? In any case, metaphors are mirrors in which we observe ourselves and windows through which our colleagues can gaze.

Lakoff and Johnson (1980) called our attention to the importance of examining our language to more fully understand our beliefs and values. They show how metaphors can illuminate our assumptions about everyday actions and roles. For instance, images of "professionalizing" the role of teacher can be examined through a lens that portrays schools as factories and teachers, therefore, as factory hands. Teachers themselves, however, are seldom asked how they see themselves and their roles. When they are asked, interesting images are presented. We value strategies for metaphorical thinking for many reasons. Metaphor is valued for its role in guiding reflection, for its ability to cross artistic and visual expression with writing, and for its role in uncovering assumptions about the profession and professional development (Cooper, Collay, & Day, 1995). Notions of "professional" are instructive, as evident in the metaphors below. Preservice and early years' teachers often see themselves in the stereotyped roles of a gardener (who nurtures children) or a craftsperson such as a mechanic (with a full toolbox of strategies). After several years' practice, however, teachers are more likely to portray their role as chaotic and unsettled and with problems that are not so simply solved.

These teachers drew a portrayal of themselves and then wrote a description of their picture. The depictions indicate the role of teacher is multifaceted and complex. The two themes of multiple roles in the classroom and balancing school with family were central. In the first excerpt, Elizabeth drew a daisy in simple strokes of a marking pen. She writes:

> I am like a flower—(daisy)—each petal representing a part of my multifaceted life. The petals are my profession, family, classroom, friends! Each petal also represents the variables in teaching (listener, learner, facilitator, substitute mother, planner, negotiator, worker, team member).

Elizabeth's description is fairly matter of fact. She assumes that it is her task to balance these many facets of her life and teaching. The two dimensions described in her text reflect each other, as the first list of four things includes professional and personal, first one then the other. Elizabeth is a substitute mother in her role as teacher and has a family at home to care for while she is a teacher.

Anna depicted her role as one of meteorologist. Her choice describes the unpredictable nature of teaching and how one can make guesses about the weather, yet remain unsure until the day is done:

> I have been focusing on climate in my class for the first quarter of the school year. Every day, the students come in and I interpret their "forecast." Where are the highs? the lows? Where is the storm front? the warm sunshine? Then I have to try to prepare everyone for my "forecast" or schedule so we can be prepared for the day and "dress for the weather." The hard part is leaving my day at school so I don't predict the next day's weather too far in advance.

Anna's choice of "highs" and "lows" reminds us that children's bodies and minds, each with their daily biorhythms, are sent from all over town into our classrooms. Teachers can only guess what might be happening through experience, having observed similar patterns, and then take steps to respond. The second theme that is pervasive throughout the metaphors in this study is the challenge to balance work and family. In Anna's case, leaving work at work and home at home proves difficult; while at home, she is challenged to make an accurate forecast.

The third excerpt was contributed by Fatima, whose sketch portrays a wide-eyed face with eight different hats flying above it. Each hat is shaped differently. For instance, the "student hat" is shaped like a mortarboard. The list also includes "ski hat, presiding hat, teacher hat, wife hat, mommy hat, and wizard hat." The hats seem to represent a fairly equal balance between her personal life and her professional life. Fatima reflected:

> I am the "hat wearer." Each day, I wear many hats and must decide when each should be worn and for how long. It is often a difficult decision, especially when more than one hat needs to be worn at a time, as they sometimes clash.

Again, the multiple roles are portrayed and the professional and personal responsibilities are given equal weight. We can imagine which roles are clashing: In the case of an after-school or evening committee meeting, the presiding hat and the mommy hat might clash as she arranges child care for her family. Like Anna, she is in a constant struggle to balance work and home.

Moving along the multiple roles and responsibilities toward more chaotic settings, Sarah portrays her role as a special education teacher for severely handicapped adolescents as "air traffic controller":

> Being a teacher in my MSMI (moderate to severe mentally impaired) classroom is like being an air traffic controller, in a way. It's sometimes life and death responsibility, almost always hectic, full of unexpected events and interruptions, ever active, stressful, and joyful. It involves the cooperation and collaboration of many—but it feels, ultimately, like "the buck stops here." I need to constantly direct (despite trying to empower) my kids, teaching assistants, and peer-parent volunteers.

Having spent time in Sarah's room, we can understand her choice of metaphor clearly. Because of the dire health conditions of her charges, this teacher is "on" in a way mainstream teachers are not. Sarah's close calls occur every hour of every day, much like the jet planes managed by an air traffic controller. She has the added challenge of a complex adult staff to supervise, monitor, and evaluate. Her sketch combines the arm waving of a conductor with cartoonlike balloons filled with orders: "I'll help you in a second—need to make sure so-and-so is safe!" and so forth.

In this final presentation, Terry has sketched a pinball machine, combining the chaos of multiple roles with the bouncing balls hurtling across the game board:

Some days I hit the "high score" and win a bonus ball. . . . More often, unfortunately, I feel as if I am bouncing from one idea to another (in terms of planning) and rarely rest in one place long enough to follow an idea through to completion. I'm left in the TILT mode too often. I'd like to learn the game better. . . .

Terry and her colleagues see their days as filled with multiple people, roles, and responsibilities. Their process of documenting reflection began with images of the profession that were not teachers (meteorologist, air traffic controller), moved into the creation of an accompanying text in which they explained their choice of metaphor, and ultimately became a tool for understanding the stresses and strains of daily life. The metaphor chosen reveals a view of self and profession that is instructive. If teachers are to transform themselves, their students, and education, they must first know where they stand and for what they stand. After personal and professional grounding, the next steps toward choice making and path choosing can be taken.

JOURNALING

We define the process of "journaling" as the act of keeping a journal for reflection. Both the word "journal" and the word "journey" come from the same Latin root, *diurna*, for "daily portion." Jotting one's thoughts on bits of paper, keeping a spiral notebook in a breast pocket, writing letters or e-mailing friends, or investing in disciplined daily writing are all ways of marking our daily journey. When we hear the word journal, we may think of the latter activity, and if we do any less, consider ourselves nonjournalists. Not every teacher will like the same reflection process, just as none of us or our students learn in exactly the same way. Here are some teachers' reactions to journaling activities. Charles found it a positive experience:

Reflecting through journal writing has also been a meaningful experience. The act of writing has been a great way to organize and articulate our thoughts and feelings, therefore bringing clarity where there was previously clutter. As we read through and [reflect on] our journals, we found them to be a good record of our learning.

For those of us who enjoy journaling as a form of reflection and assessment, these remarks strike a familiar chord. As with our students, however, we must be sympathetic to and respectful of those who don't find one method of assessment to their liking. Sally could have done without it:

> I did not care for the journaling process as a means of documenting my reflection of my progress as a learner and a teacher. I found the idea of journaling to be an artificial means of self-communication. I didn't enjoy it and did not get used to doing it at any time.

There are two things to remember in organizing a professional development program or choosing as a learning circle to do reflective activities: First, it may be an unfamiliar process for some people and it may take some time for them to understand the long-term value of reflective practice on their own learning. Second, some people learn better by talking through the process rather than writing it down. What we have encouraged participants to do in this case is to record or otherwise document their oral reflections, so they are still participating in reflection on their own learning. Using short lists, poems, sketches, one-sentence statements, or other creative reflections to create a record is more efficient than the prose of long journal entries.

REFLECTING WITH COLLEAGUES

We have learned in our work with portfolio assessment that merely gathering artifacts, articles, and ideas does not a portfolio make. In Chapter 6, we discuss the importance of conducting appropriate assessment in the context of a learning circle or any setting of trusted colleagues. The colleague group offers a forum in which individuals can make sense of what they might use and how they might use materials to portray their professional identity. Ultimately, however, the decision about choosing the material for the portfolio is a deeply individual one.

This teacher reviewed materials she had gathered over a school year. In her reflections, she finally made sense of the patterns in those materials. Her portfolio is a tapestry—many threads organized in a beautiful portrayal of a professional:

> I have titled my portfolio "A Tapestry of Learning." If one looks at the back of a piece of tapestry, there are thousands of different colored threads going every which way in no apparent pattern. For a person like me who appreciates order, the back of a tapestry is simply not very beautiful. Often, during the last 9 months, I have felt the exact same way about my portfolio. It was bits and pieces of things I had done that were supposed to symbolize my learning, but I did not see how they fit together. When I looked at it, it seemed like an unorganized mess and I wondered if I had really learned anything at all.
>
> My view of my portfolio shifted when I decided to sit down and reflect on myself and my learning. I thought about myself as a learner and I began to choose artifacts that symbolized the things I felt I had learned this year. The act of making my portfolio truly mine was an exciting experience. It was as if the tapestry had been turned over to reveal the beautifully rich pattern on the other side.

In our classrooms and in our staff development activities, we often find ourselves expressing the same sentiments as Nancy. We read an article, we capture a workshop, or we bring back a document with directions on how to teach. We might wonder, "Have I learned anything?" Our students feel the same way—bells ring through the building, signaling the end of a learning experience, and, often, there has been no formal, deliberate acknowledgment of what has been learned, how we will apply it later, why it was there to be learned. Only through reflection can we begin to make sense of those many threads that make up the fabric of our learning and our lives. And only by documenting reflection can we make it accessible for colleagues and open our reflection for review and feedback.

STRUCTURED REFLECTION

Documenting reflection can be as open-ended or structured as the learning circle thinks is useful. Choices about documentation should reflect the purpose of the task. Some reflections are very personal and open to individual interpretation. Others can take people through a very structured process of reflection. In this example, how we come to know something and our assumptions about what we already know are outlined in a structured manner.

MAPS stands for *m*odels, *a*rguments, *p*urposes, and *s*tructures. These categories can be used to analyze and document a learning event and to make cultural assumptions about learning explicit. This model is based on the work of David Perkins and his colleagues (1986) in Project Zero, where the focus was on developing ways to describe things, events, or behaviors before we "name" them. We have used variations on this exercise to stimulate reflection on, discussion about, and documentation of our assumptions about culture and to point to aspects of our culture that we might like to change or modify. We have also used the model to help explain why a particular cultural behavior might be resistant to change, even when we are trying to change it.

The facilitator first prints the four categories M, A, P, S as headings on four sheets of chart paper or on a board. The facilitator can cite Perkins (1986) and use his examples as illustrations. Perkins's first example was a thumbtack. The model can be an actual thumbtack and the question, "Why is the head so wide?" or "Why is the point so short?" The purpose is to temporarily attach materials to a surface. The structure is short point, wide head. The facilitator can then say, "You can see how changing the assumption in any category might alter the next design."

Ask the participants what might be different about their description of the MAPS categories if the behavior being analyzed was from an adult or from a small child. The child counting pebbles in Chapter 3 is an example. What if an adult were counting pebbles on the ground? Another example might be how different your reactions would be if a 5-year-old showed you he could count his toes and name them or if a 50-year-old proudly showed you the same thing. Ask why there are differences in what we see as "appropriate" or "marvelous" behavior simply related to age.

Ask the participants to change one of the MAPS categories in a radical way, and then ask what the effect would be. Ask why. Use Perkins's (1986) example of a thumbtack. Change the purpose from temporary attachment to a surface to permanent attachment. Another example would be to use a cotton swab but say the item is made of wood instead of cotton, or metal instead of wood. Or, make it for cleaning the ears of a big dog or cow. Members of the learning circle can brainstorm the most radical modification they can think of and then work with the consequences of the one chosen from the brainstorming. The idea is to show how one change in one part of the system alters the whole system and may produce a very different effect. Capturing individual and group reflection on these learning activities moves the effort from a disconnected task to a learning event among other contextualized and meaningful actions.

This same process can be used to analyze artifacts from a previous activity, to analyze or predict a current political event, to classify slang, or to look at strategic planning in history. If cultural understanding and learning are the focus of the activity, it is useful to appoint "culture" and "learning" monitors and ask them to report to the whole group at the end of the activity. Ask them to use the MAPS categories or the six conditions in taking their notes and they will not be left out of the activity even though they are participating in a different way. Their careful documentation will be available for the membership.

REFLECTION FOR PROGRAM EVALUATION

Program evaluation is often seen by educators as a necessary evil. We believe that external assessment can provide a valuable framework for individual and group reflection. Diane recently worked with a teaching staff at an Indian K-12 school where the staff sought to turn an evaluation "problem" into an opportunity for group reflection and that reflection became a centerpiece for staff members committed to improving their practice:

> Last year, I got a call from our friend and colleague, P. J. Ford-Slack. She had been working with the staff in a small school in the northern part of the state that was undergoing federal program evaluation. The new rules were a case study in the latest thinking about theory-based program evaluation—lots of questionnaires and interviews, protocols, and multiple points of assessment. I didn't see much awareness of how hard these would be to complete in a reservation school. The protocol didn't fit the setting or the people.

We sorted the evaluation requirements into three piles: things we could do easily, things that were absurd, and things that might be useful with some modification. We convened a representative group of the whole staff and community for a long work retreat and worked our way through each category. We had the group break into small groups and asked them to reflect on how the evaluation requirements fit the mission statement (covenant) they had created the year before. As reflections were shared, ideas began to come forward about how to work with one or another of the difficult requirements. By the end of the second work retreat, any member of the group could describe the overall plan to people outside the group. Each person could explain why the questions were being asked and how they fit the mission statement of the school and the goals for the year. They had taken what could have been a real problem and through reflection and collaboration turned the process into another learning opportunity for everyone.

Program evaluation, even when externally imposed, is a natural opportunity for members of an organization to reflect on covenants, missions, and goals as a "process history." Using good group process, a school staff or learning circles can pose the questions, "How will we know that we have achieved our goals?" and "How will we demonstrate our accomplishments to others?" Professionals can and must take ownership of their development, especially in the face of externally imposed mandates.

REFLECTION WITHIN LEARNING CIRCLES

Each of the authors can identify learning circles in which documentation of the group's process was central to the activity. A scribe shapes the record and other members benefit from seeing their words in print and their ideas acknowledged in a tangible fashion. Reflections of professionals also offer a teaching text for others. In the preface, we spoke about Perrone, Duckworth, Carini, and others who created learning circles and carefully wrote down the reflections that grew from those groups so that other educators might benefit from their experiences. In many of our other examples, the power of the small group to function for its members and to influence the greater community of learners often lies in the group's ability to capture its members' learning and meaning making and then transmit that to the larger community. The learning circle itself functions best when individuals have time to reflect. It improves individual and collective thinking, and it improves the quality of the interaction with others in the circle. Learning circles are often called on to mediate the new learning that individuals or other learning circles undertake—and careful documentation is central to their success.

As Schon (1983) suggests, professionals must "discover and restructure the interpersonal theories of action" (p. 353). We believe they will find the most success with this endeavor by building their theories of action together in the company of other like-minded practitioners.

FOR FURTHER READING

Brookfield, S. (1990). Using critical incidents to explore learners' assumptions. In J. Mezirow and Associates (Eds.), *Fostering critical reflection in adulthood: A guide to transformative and emancipatory learning.* San Francisco: Jossey-Bass.

Hoshmand, L. (1993). The personal narrative in the communal construction of self and life issues. In G. Neimeyer (Ed.), *Constructivist assessment: A casebook.* Newbury Park, CA: Sage.

CHAPTER SIX

ASSESSING EXPECTATIONS

Play also creates the zone of proximal development in the child. In play, the child is always behaving beyond his age, above his usual everyday behavior; in play he is, as it were, always a head above himself.

Lev Vygotsky
(quoted in Van Der Veer
& Valsiner, 1991, p. 345)

Many species use play to learn new behaviors and test knowledge in a safe setting. Play is seen as something that is for children, however, rather than adults. We often define child and adult by using these words: Children play and adults work. Thinking about learning as play rather than work allows us to imagine new possibilities for personal growth and professional development. Then, we can recreate the conditions necessary to learn new knowledge by experimentation and play. Most "techie" computer nerds approach a new program playfully, much the way a child does a video game. They try out menus and functions of a program with an attitude of "Let's see what this will do" rather than being limited by a manual that tells them in a deliberate and slow way. What if assessment were seen as a safe way for teachers to test new knowledge about teaching and learning?

Unfortunately, assessment often reflects a judgmental stance toward learners. We hear the term *assessment* and think, "Who wants to assess and for what are they looking?" This kind of thinking might stimulate us, but it also limits what we can hope to learn. Self-assessment is often seen as less important or critical than evaluation by an objective judge. Diane recalled the following story while reflecting on the relationship between assessment and expectations she had of herself, her daughter, and the role of educational culture in limiting who she was or could become:

I took many years of assessment and evaluation courses as part of my doctoral and postdoctoral studies in education. I subsequently taught research and evaluation techniques over two decades of faculty work and served on numerous thesis and dissertation committees where some form of assessment was an essential part of the research. I served as a third-party evaluator on the effectiveness of several national education projects. However, I learned the most about the deepest conflicts embedded in the process of assessment from my daughter, Claire.

During her school years, Claire was variously classified as "damaged," "dyslexic," and "trainable mentally retarded." She presented a challenge to teachers. While she could perform at grade level in some subjects, she was always many levels behind in other subjects. Her math papers, for example, usually came home with a sea of red checks on them and were usually accompanied with a request for another parent-teacher conference to review her "performance." By the time she graduated from high school, I had a three-drawer file cabinet filled with the many tests, grades, and evaluations given to her over the years as we sought methods that would help her the most.

One day during her sixth-grade year, after another round of difficult tests, I asked her what purpose she thought tests and grades served. She replied, "The tests are to prove to the teachers what I don't know. They believe I can't learn, and the tests prove it for them." Stunned by her reply, I asked her if she agreed with the tests. She looked at me as if I had said something truly funny, and she laughed. "Of course not," she exclaimed. "You know I can learn! I learn a lot every day, but nobody asks me on a test what I can do or what I know. They mostly ask me what I don't know." "How could they find out what you can do and what you know?" I asked. "They could ask me," she said, "but they never do. Tests are to prove to other people that I am not as good as other students, and it is not the teacher's fault if I don't learn something. Tests don't really have anything to do with who I am and what I know."

Claire had unknowingly identified the critical difference between assessment against expectations set by others and assessment for one's own expectations. It is the difference between actual learning and the process of being schooled. Although few educators would be happy with Claire's conclusions about testing, her reasoning was sound. She hit on the truth about assessment: It makes a big difference who is doing it, why it is being done, and how the learner is involved.

BELIEFS ABOUT ASSESSMENT

So often we assume that students understand why we give tests and use other forms of evaluation. We tell ourselves and our students that no one should equate self-worth with how well someone does on a particular test, but we use the results of tests and grades to rank the "best" and "worst" of "performance." Although our nation is built on notions of equity and fairness, it is also a competitive society where some "succeed" and some "fail."

So, what does this have to do with learning circles? It is important to use assessment techniques and procedures that support individual and group learning. Unfortunately, not all assessment processes support learning. For example, if a teacher wants to make sure that students understand the lessons taught in a particular week, the teacher will probably review the lessons before and after teaching and then give a test based on the lessons. Instead of guessing how well each student has learned the lesson material, the teacher has documentation. This process reassures most of us that we have moved away from intuitive reaction to something more scientific and reliable.

Another example of assessment as scientific documentation can be seen in the evaluation of teachers. If a principal wants to assess the teaching skills of a particular teacher, she might discuss or negotiate what kind of observation to make, make the observation, and then discuss the findings afterward. The results might be used as a learning exercise for principal and teacher or might be used in making a formal determination of annual performance. If the teacher believes that retaining his position depends on how the principal perceives the observed teaching event, he is likely to try and show the best teaching skills possible. If the principal is a master teacher who has sufficient observation time to get a fair understanding of the teacher's classroom practice, the teacher may engage fully, take risks, and learn from the evaluation. If the principal knows little about teaching, does not discuss the way in which teaching is being judged, spends little time observing the teacher, and then uses the results to determine merit, the teacher may be less engaged and is unlikely to learn better teaching skills from the process. The teacher is unlikely to display what he perceives as his weakest skill—even though a skilled evaluator may be able to help the teacher improve that skill by coaching feedback.

Assessment techniques and processes have been grounded in one of the most basic tenets of scientism: The way to distinguish between "beliefs" and "facts" is to structure data collection around predetermined, scientifically valid goals and hypotheses. This approach assumes that desired knowledge exists outside the learner and is selected by the teacher/leader who also decides if the learner has learned properly. This is not a constructivist process.

APPROPRIATE ASSESSMENT

In selecting appropriate assessment methods for the individual learner and for the learning circle, individuals or groups must establish the purpose of assessment. Is the assessment focused only on meeting expectations or is it focused on how participants have tried to change in an effort to accomplish the agreed-on expectations? For example, if the mathematics department in a high school is asked by the district to adopt the National Council of Teachers of Mathematics (NCTM) math standards, its members have some options about how they will assess their success with that task. If they agree that a 3-year adoption cycle that includes attending training sessions and working with a consultant is useful, they can document those efforts along with the students' scores. Assessment of professional development is necessary for growth.

Will the assessment be used to determine the quality of the learning event rather than focusing on outcomes alone? Mihaly Csikszentmihalyi (1990) has described the psychological state of optimal experience as a state of "flow." "Flow" is when we are so completely engaged in a task or experience that it commands our complete attention, and all of our senses and mental acuity are directed into the experience. People often report losing any sense of time during an optimal experience. They also recall the experience as refreshing and relaxing as well as completely engaging. Athletes often refer to a state of "flow" as "being in the zone," when everything appears clear and moving more slowly so they can almost see what to do next. For learning to be an optimal experience, the learner cannot be worried about "making a mistake." Instead of thinking in terms of mistakes, optimal experience encourages experimentation in seeking what most supports the learner engaged in a learning event. Can you imagine an assessment being a "flow" experience?

In addition to choosing appropriate assessment and considering the learning process as well as the learning outcome, the timing of assessment is critical. One of the quickest ways to stifle the experimental or playful impulse that opens us to new learning is to impose a summative "test" or judgment on the learning event before we are secure in our new knowledge. It may not be the type of test or judgment that closes us to psychological optimal experience or the testing itself. Instead, it might be the way in which the testing process is administered and how the individual or group perceives the psychological and social impact of the test. For example, a world-class runner may rise to new levels of performance during a race. The fact that there is a judgment in the race, in the form of how well the runner places, may add to the challenge instead of decreasing the sense of flow. For a flow state to occur under these circumstances, however, typically means that the runner has already practiced with different techniques, pacing patterns, footwear, and so on before the race and has already discovered the new knowledge that leads to the optimal event. In other words, the conditions necessary for optimal new learning have already occurred before the race and have been integrated by the runner into the knowledge available to the runner during the race. The "test" becomes a chance to reach for new performance "success" instead of proof of "failure."

To lessen the effects of the embedded culture of schooling, with assessments as terminal judgment of our worth, it may be productive for a learning circle to experiment with a completely different set of assumptions about assessing learning. One way to do this is to adopt David Bohm's (1981) theory of implicate order. What would learning and assessment look like if each of us already contained all possible learning outcomes—including the outcome of perfect, complete learning—and all activities that we do are aimed at uncovering the embedded perfection that already exists within us? What kinds of things would you say to a fellow learner under this assumption? How would you say it? Brainstorming as a group about what learning might look like under this assumption can help the learning circle members see more clearly the effects of learning or assessment that are not aimed at learning. It can help the members see the deeply embedded cultural notions of schooling, particularly where they can interfere with learning.

APPROACHES TO ASSESSMENT

Recall the last driver's license examination where you had an "opportunity" to show what you could or could not do on a written test and in a car. Someone else decided if you passed the test. The decision to grant (or not grant) the license was made by the examiner and was based on your performance. At the end of the test, you knew what you did right and what you did wrong. We hope you got enough items right so that you got the license—but you didn't set your own assessment goals and processes.

Most assessment is a form of *summative* evaluation like the teacher testing of the student, the principal observing teaching for annual performance evaluation, or the driving examination. The assessment is done to determine if the person being tested has learned "enough" to "pass." Based on this form of assessment, most of us learn to dislike making an "error" or "mistake" and see errors as failures on our part. If our goal is to establish a framework for learning new things, however, summative assessment is not useful, and leads us into cul-de-sacs of limitations rather than onto highways opening in many directions.

Another approach to assessment is *formative* evaluation. Examples include testing of knowledge or skills in order to be placed at an appropriate level for learning, such as testing of skiing skills for placement in a ski class or testing of language skills to determine the appropriate level for additional learning. Typically, "pass" or "fail" does not apply in formative testing; the testing process is simply to determine what the person knows at the time of the test. One cannot make mistakes or errors in formative testing; instead of an "error," a gap in knowledge or skill simply indicates where to begin learning.

There are significant similarities and differences between these two types of assessment, particularly when we focus on learning.

What best supports learners in a learning circle is determined by the goals set by the individual learner, by the circle itself, by the greater community, and by any outside agency making any type of performance judgment. These goals may or may not be compatible. For example, an individual teacher in a learning circle may want to focus on becoming more comfortable with alternative teaching strategies. The teacher may discuss what kind of activities she wants to do individually and what kinds of activities will be done in the learning circle. The appropriate assessment technique may be as simple as documentation of the processes followed and a self-assessment of whether the teacher has reached the desired new comfort level. Because the individual is a member of a supportive learning circle, she may choose to share the process to be followed in advance of the learning and then share the self-determined results of the activities completed. The learning circle may choose to have successful completion of this individual goal counted as part of the overall assessment of the learning circle's success.

If learning circle members choose to learn something together, the process of setting the learning goal begins by determining in advance how progress against the goal will be documented and when and how the circle will formally assess its progress toward the goal. Most evaluation processes can be adapted to serve this type of communal goal. Learning circles can draft their own "test," which they will give their members at a preselected date. A learning circle might choose to bring in people from outside the circle to observe members' skills. Or, a learning circle may decide to set aside times for members to assess progress for themselves.

SELF-ASSESSMENT

So, how does one select assessment methods that produce the desired result? The cycle of assessment is best served by a progression of self-assessment, learning circle assessment, and then large group or external assessment. Beginning with external demands does not allow a high-quality assessment process to emerge. The core questions to ask are "What most serves the goals of learning? What are appropriate assessment conditions for the learner and the learning circle?" Begin with self-assessment and ask the following questions:

- Under what conditions of assessment do I feel most comfortable?

- Under what conditions do I learn the most?

- Have I had negative testing or evaluation experiences in the past?

- What about the experience was negative for me?

- What kinds of assessment can I do that give me good feedback on my learning but do not recreate negative experiences?

Addressing these self-assessment questions should be part of the expectation-setting process early in the formation of the learning circle. This activity is the first stepping-stone of assessment history for each learner. Each learner has experienced many assessment events in the past; reviewing them and learning what works best for the individual is a key first step in selecting assessment processes that will work for the learning circle.

In an elementary school, for example, a team of second-grade teachers might form a learning circle around the goal of expanding their strategies for the teaching of reading. Three of the four teachers agree to attend a workshop on choosing literature for second-language speakers to improve the acquisition of English. The fourth may be more interested in creating writing workshops for his students. They agree to discuss appropriate literature each week at their circle meetings, but they also agree to support the single member in his pursuit of writing workshop curriculum. They decide to invite their English as a Second Language specialist to attend their circle to offer support, critique, and methods by which they can evaluate their students' progress.

The next step in selecting appropriate and supportive assessment processes for individuals and a learning circle is for members to share assumptions about assessment with the other members. Listen closely as fellow learners share their experiences. Often, additional memories and reactions will come up during this process. Steve had this to say about self-assessment in relation to professional development activities:

> I am a more reflective person now. I liked being able to personalize my learning and share what the information means to me. I have done this with my students. We can always go to books or

computers and find the right answer, but isn't it more important to be able to tell what the information means to me, the learner?

There was evidence that teachers in our program were challenged by creating their own forms of assessment—like students, many would have preferred that someone else set standards and give instructions for meeting those standards. Over time, however, the membership came to value the autonomy and efficacy that self-designed and learning circle-designed assessment brought each of them.

Individual teachers and learning circles must also respond to external demands for assessment, but large groups such as faculties or classes can also make choices about their assessment processes. As professionals, most of us are willing to try ideas that may not seem a good fit or a first choice. It is not necessary to reject these assessment activities simply because they do not serve all learners; they simply become assessment activities that are used primarily for those learners they support. One of the guidelines to use in sorting individual testing methods from those used by the whole group is to identify methods that have produced negative experiences for any learning circle members. If the leaders have the choice, they should not use those that have proved negative experiences for the whole group or at least limit how they are used. Separate these methods from other kinds of assessment and invite the group to propose more constructive forms of evaluation for individuals and the group. In classrooms, students might be invited to think about how they would like to be assessed and by whom. In an elementary art program in a suburban school, the art teacher sets up an art show each spring. The students help determine the criteria by which their work will be judged. At each step in the creation of the painting or sculpture, they judge their own work against those criteria (a formative evaluation strategy). They select an entry to submit based on that knowledge, undergo a judging process, and conduct a final self-evaluation at the exhibit (summative evaluation). Their learning far exceeds the creation of a picture.

PEER ASSESSMENT

Peer assessment is an important method of positive collaborative evaluation in learning circles. It is important to model nonintervention, sharing without judgment, and sharing with supportive judgment. Initial expectation setting should be conducted by the individual learner, then by the learning circle. Members should also consider implied expectations in any assessment processes that may be imposed on the learning circle or the larger community. The processes used for assessment of progress should be discussed and agreed to by members of the learning circle in advance of the learning events themselves. There are several methods that we have found to be very effective in creating conditions for learning through positive assessment activities. Here are other examples of peer assessment that are positive and productive.

Six high school English teachers brainstorm ways to assess their individual and collective learning about using the fine arts to teach great works. They plan to assess their learning by documenting how they selected appropriate songs or musical scores for plays they teach, where they found paintings or drawings of characters from books, and why they chose a musical such as *West Side Story*, a modern-day version of *Romeo and Juliet*. They determine the following criteria: Each teacher will identify one item in each category, review the item for usefulness with the students and courses, and review one other member's work. They agree to design appropriate assessment of the students' learning and pilot-test it over the term, making modifications where necessary.

A grade-level team of teachers decides to implement a math manipulative curriculum. Each member of the team agrees to try two of the manipulatives available, interview the students about their learning, rate the materials for usefulness and match with the textbook, and report back to the team. They agree to select the most useful and recommend purchase of more materials to their principal. The four teachers' reviews will be collected and shared with the full staff at the next faculty development session.

Each member of a junior high school faculty agrees to identify one other colleague who will engage in a cognitive coaching exchange. The dyads agree to draw up an evaluation process, use it during peer reviews, and conduct follow-up conversations. The evaluation frameworks will be submitted to an evaluation committee of peers who will design a new teaching evaluation rubric.

Creating conditions for supporting learners in community means attending to individual needs and differences. If personal growth needs are not met, professional development goals will not be met. If attention is paid to personal differences in selecting assessment methods, then assessment will be seen as an organic, interactive, and positive part of the overall learning experience.

PORTFOLIO ASSESSMENT

Colleague support is critical in the development of portfolios. Personal interactions lie at the heart of professional exchanges about learning. The development of individual portfolios takes place inside peer review groups or learning circles. At each meeting, groups work together to interpret and delineate the curriculum and evaluations for the small group and individuals within it. Out of these conversations grow assessment frameworks reflecting both the core requirements of the program and outcomes for the five propositions from the NBPTS (1991). Evaluation frameworks for applied research projects were designed by the learning circles.

The learning circles played a critical role in establishing a forum for conversations about portfolios. For a school staff undertaking portfolio assessment, we suggest such groups be developed during the first 3 months of a school year, when members can create peer advisory groups or learning circles. They can focus on grade-level teams, interest areas, or mixed groups working toward curriculum goals. Professionals are more motivated to work with schoolwide or districtwide efforts if their individual contributions and needs are acknowledged.

Wolf, Whinery, and Hagerty (1995) present their ideas about teaching portfolios with particular attention to the "structured conversations" that support the portfolio development and review process. The authors suggest that these conversations are most productive when they focus on the improvement of an individual's teaching, rather than on teaching or education in general. The authors emphasize the importance of the study group or learning circle in which the portfolio is presented. The conversation guide suggests that the portfolio author:

1. Present a teaching artifact(s)
2. Pose questions for the group to consider

3. Discuss various teaching and learning approaches with the group in light of the questions asked and the information conveyed through the artifacts

4. Consider questions raised by other group members

5. Comment on what was learned and what action will be taken (p. 35)

Leaders in the position to set the norms for assessment should consider the use of portfolios for professionals. One approach is to use the adopted goals of the individual and the learning circle to establish a learning portfolio. This can be as simple as a file folder with the goals listed on a sheet of paper or a computer file dedicated to the selected goal. We find that using plastic filing bins with hanging file folders keyed to the goals of the individual, the learning circle, and the community allowed an individualized learning portfolio to develop over the time. As exercises, reflections, and group events are documented, the participant can begin to see a pattern of learning occurring. The portfolios can be all-inclusive or can be sorted in a more selective manner at certain points in the process. The unedited, complete learning portfolio can be private or shared with other members of the learning circle. An edited selective portfolio can be an excellent way to demonstrate to people outside the learning circle what learning has been occurring in the circle. It can also be an informative learning process for the circle as circle members reflect on what types of documentation best demonstrates learning. Vito Perrone (1991) has advocated for appropriate assessments in schools. He reminds us that such assessment has a larger history:

> The kind of record keeping that makes up what is currently called documentation, the types of work that fill a portfolio, and the projects that are the basis for what we now call performance assessments or exhibits of learning were common in many 19th century schools and were basic to practices in numerous progressive schools. (p. viii)

The image of a visual artist with a large cardboard satchel is a useful one for those who have not done portfolio assessment before. Imagine an artist painting many pictures over several years and collecting them in such a satchel. The artist is then asked to meet with a gallery director to choose one picture for an upcoming exhibit. The artist must select those specific paintings he or she believes are appropriate for that director at that gallery for that event. Only those paintings that meet those criteria are taken to the meeting. Together, the two professionals debate the merits of each painting. Finally, they choose one that best meets the criteria for that exhibit.

George and Michelle worked with the Early Childhood Committee in Minneapolis Public Schools to develop portfolio assessment strategies for teachers of primary-grade literacy. From that collaboration emerged the following categories, which we now use to guide our own portfolio development and that of others with whom we work:

1. *Collect.* Keep everything until you know what you will use and for which criteria. Make initial categories related to individual expectations, learning circle expectations, and external expectations. Don't panic about the ambiguity of the categories!

2. *Select.* Choose which collected pieces to keep. Compare categories again and add or subtract categories as they emerge or fade. Keep anything you feel demonstrates your learning, knowing you can set it aside later.

3. *Reflect.* After making the initial selection, review the criteria you used. Why did you select particular pieces? What do they show about your learning? What will you do with everything else? Can you imagine different settings in which you might make different choices?

4. *Inspect.* Build a plan for portfolio review. Who will see it and how will you show it? Which materials exemplify what kind of learning? Do you want to show progress over time (formative evaluation) or just the final product (summative evaluation)?

Celebrate your accomplishments with your learning circle. The four stages of portfolio development described above require a commitment of time and energy. Exposing one's work to colleagues is also a risk. Take time to celebrate.

When we first introduced the development of professional portfolios of teacher work to groups of teachers, we heard lots of complaints based on confusion and fear. Working in unknown territory requires trust and a willingness to teach and reteach the steps in advance so people are not shaken by the perceived lack of structure. With time and support, development of a portfolio is a cause for celebration, as Bob reflects:

> My portfolio has become a continuing picture of the kind of educator I am. I am proud of my portfolio for many reasons. . . . It shows my dedication to my school, colleagues, students, and the parents I conference with. I don't plan on moving and having to get another job, but I know how invaluable a portfolio can be. I will continue to put updated materials in it.

These next remarks demonstrate the need for teachers to engage in such assessment practice before attempting to lead their students through it. Rachelle recalled:

> For the first time, I was able to thoroughly reflect on myself professionally by creating a "brag book" that represented me! It helped my self-esteem and confidence to see my accomplishments in one project. The affirmations of colleagues strengthened my pride for myself in education. I brought my portfolio in to my classroom and shared it with my students. They were glad that I experienced the concept before asking them to create a portfolio of their own.

There is a clear sense of accomplishment in these statements. We find it remarkable that the simple act of taking time to look at one's accomplishment provides so much validation! Teachers' chronic struggle for time may be even more insidious than merely depriving their students of high-quality learning. They are starved for professional interactions necessary for their own learning. These next observations reflect the connection of the portfolio to an external (NBPTS, 1991) assessment framework. Koua gave this description:

> The process of constructing my portfolio was a long and tedious one at times, but as it was assembled and categorized according to the NBPTS. I gained insight as to what was important to me as an educator, and it validated my teaching practices. I am proud of what I have accomplished and hope in the future to expand on what I have done [in my portfolio]. I don't see it as an

end [but] as a process that will be revisited and continually evaluated in the future.

We listed many comments about the portfolio process because much of our learning about the significance of this assessment process came directly from teachers finding their unique ways through the process. We have seen as many types of good, illustrative portfolios as we have seen professionals undertaking them. We have been particularly struck by the depth of analysis brought to discussions of teaching and portfolios after completing this process. We believe that a thorough portfolio process is essential to mastering understanding of what it means to be a good and unique teacher.

CHANGING THE CULTURE OF ASSESSMENT

Another important role of the learning circle is to articulate assumptions about assessment. Throughout the development of the portfolios, learning circle members rely on each other for feedback and direction as each takes new paths to self and small group assessment. And, like other groups mentioned in this book, the learning circle provided the forum to experiment with and to mediate more appropriate methods of assessment. Kelly mirrors what many feel about assessment:

> The methods of assessing teachers in this program worked out well for me. I experienced an entirely new look at assessment, which I was not comfortable with at first. All of my experience as a student has been to read or work out problems and then take a test. That is what I am used to, comfortable with, and good at. This program has shown me that I can be assessed in other ways and still do fine. . . . I can also assess myself. I am much more comfortable with the idea of change. In fact, I am anxious to discover ways that are more useful, practical, and meaningful than old paradigm methods.

Kelly felt that a thorough examination of assessment had been useful to his own development. Sheila describes another aspect critical to school reform and changing cultures—the actual participation in a way of learning, subsequent realizations, and the discomfort one experiences while navigating that change:

> The most significant thing that we learned through this experience was realizing that constructivism works. We gained knowledge of constructivism; we experienced constructivism; and, over time, we became comfortable with learning in this model. We realized our learning was more meaningful because we set our own standards, rather than trying to meet the expectations of our instructors. However, slipping into our old habits was a common trap. We often desired a list of criteria from which to work. We wanted to work to the level expected of us by others, rather than working to meet our own criteria. The ambiguity was uncomfortable and often quite frustrating.

Many teachers struggle with changing the culture of assessment from external validation to more meaningful and appropriate self-assessment. Collectively, learning circle members can serve themselves, each other, and their schools by changing the culture of assessment.

FOR FURTHER READING

Bird, T. (1989). The schoolteacher's portfolio. In L. Darling-Hammond & J. Millman (Eds.), *Handbook on the evaluation of elementary and secondary schoolteachers.* Newbury Park, CA: Sage.

Henning-Stout, M. (1994). *Responsive assessment: A new way of thinking about learning.* San Francisco: Jossey-Bass.

CHAPTER SEVEN

CHANGING CULTURES

All that I have said implicates not only a transformation
of school as a learning culture but also the transformation
of the role of teacher in that culture—and, I suspect, the
culture at large.

Jerome Bruner
(1996, p. 85)

In the field of education, we use the term *culture* in many different ways. We agree with Bruner that schools have a learning culture; teachers have a role in that culture; and, ultimately, teachers and schools affect the culture at large. We live in communities with customs and traditions we establish, and we hold values and beliefs that are sometimes obvious and sometimes invisible. We may not think explicitly about the culture in which we live and work or realize how our work culture and life cultures relate to each other. Culture is an embedded part of how we define ourselves, yet we do not often stop to identify common beliefs, social customs, or material artifacts that may mark our culture as distinct from others; we simply act in accustomed ways. Our "reality," however, is culturally bound. What is perceived as real by one person may be very different from another person's perception of reality. Cultures also change; sometimes without obvious direction and sometimes by design. Walter describes an experience with a learning event designed to display new cultural rules:

Each summer, I work with the Concordia Language Villages in Minnesota. This program sponsors 20 language summer camps in 10 languages for over 6,000 students who are 7 to 18 years old. There are six permanent sites and a dozen borrowed sites. Each summer, the culture of a particular language must be recreated anew. At each site, the physical space is purposefully transformed with a "material culture" of authentic artifacts: objects, posters, arts, crafts, and foods. Whether the language being studied is Japanese, Swedish, or Russian, the counselors attempt to model typical rhythms and regulations of the culture. Food, music, videos, games, and other social activities and cultural traditions are used to create a cultural meaning system or to establish ways to interact in the newly formed language village.

The day the new "villagers" arrive, they use "passports" in the language of their new village to register and pass through "customs." All "contraband" (that is, anything in English such as magazines, books, or radios that might pick up local broadcasts) is confiscated. The student villagers then proceed to the village bank where their dollars are exchanged for local currency. English is only used in the following weeks as necessary for the safety or well-being of individual students.

Among the many fascinating aspects of this very successful program is how each new group of counselors and other program leaders come to a little-used camp and, in a few short weeks, create a temporary, yet realistic, Japanese, Russian, or Spanish village. New counselors work with experienced counselors. Almost all have direct experience with the culture and language of the new village. Counselors meet together before the village begins and learn about the language and culture. They continue to meet throughout the life of the language camp to compare results and to problem-solve together. The high rates of successful language learning and the enthusiasm shown by the great majority of the students for the process reflect the success achieved by deliberately recreating culture.

INTERDEPENDENT NETWORKS AND CULTURES

We see the ecological perspective of interdependent networks as a key to our theoretical thinking about cultures and change. Kegan (1982) refers to "holding environments" where developing individuals remain in a safe and secure cultural cocoon at several different phases of development until they are ready to emerge into a broader cultural system. Capra (1996) described a "web of life" where cultures and ecocultures are all interdependent in a network of human and natural ecosystems. From our perspective, the cultures of families, schools, communities, and American mass media all share related patterns of action through a broad interdependent network and are difficult to isolate because of mutual interest and influence.

Linda Lambert and her colleagues (1995) offered such an integrated ecological perspective when she described the key ideas that informed her work on constructivist leadership:

1. The lives of children and adults are inextricably intertwined.
2. Constructivism is the primary basis of learning for children, adults, and organizations.
3. Communities that encourage the growth of human potential are based on ecology.
4. Patterns of relationships form the primary bases for human growth and development.
5. Diversity provides complexity, depth, and multiple perspectives to relationships, thereby extending human and societal possibilities. (pp. xi-xii)

Lambert's approach to leadership reflects these assumptions about interdependent networks of cultures in individuals, organizations, and society. We find this perspective particularly helpful to understand the process of changing cultures by learning, mentoring, and leading.

UNDERSTANDING CULTURE

Educators use the term *culture* in reference to the culture of their educational organization, such as a school or district; the cultures of their community, such as race, class, or ethnicity; and the popular cultural icons such as language, music, or dance. In the case of the Concordia Language Villages, language, customs, and artifacts of the American mainstream culture are removed so that a new language with its traditional customs and artifacts can replace them.

This process also works for professionals making meaning about the culture of their organization. If teachers are to have the tools they need to understand their school culture, their role in transforming it, and their relationships to the culture at large, they need experiences and strategies for making sense of those cultures. The culture at large includes the culture of the school's community and the popular culture of mainstream America, such as sports, television, music, movies, and malls.

We offer a framework to use when examining cultures, either a familiar culture or a new one. This framework can be used to understand a school culture or a larger culture; it can be used by a newcomer or by a learning circle. As newcomers to the profession, we are encouraged to fit in; to mimic the cultural norms in place; and to not question the status quo, which we "couldn't have the experience to understand." It can also be difficult to make sense of the complex culture of the school as the embedded cultural norms that occur in other parts of our lives may be replayed in the workplace in different ways.

Walter has adapted the work of D'Andrade (1992) through the acronym *CREED* to guide discussion of culture. CREED stands for activities that are

- *C*reative
- *R*epresentative
- *E*vocative
- *E*valuative
- *D*irective

The argument is that all cultures have written and unwritten rules for each of these categories of activities.

Creative activities include learning, creating artwork, building structures, and establishing organizations. What activities are accepted as creative work? How does a culture value visual, graphic, theater, music, or dance presentations? Is cooking an art? Who are the creative people, and where do they work?

Representative activities are artifacts of the culture around us, such as books, buildings, furniture, clothing, or food. How do we move around? Where and what do we eat? How do we dress? What are the furnishings and decorations in homes and institutions?

Evocative activities are those events in the culture that evoke emotion, such as holidays, religious rituals, political actions, or sporting events. When and how is it appropriate to express emotion? What behaviors are acceptable at a football game but not acceptable in a church service? How does the culture deal with significant life events like births and deaths?

Evaluative activities are the ways a culture judges people and things. How do we determine the quality of shared practices, care, community, justice, or discipline? How do we measure the success of practices, programs, and organizations? How do we monitor capacity for change?

Directive activities include the ways in which rules are established, implemented, and enforced. Who makes the rules and how are they accepted? How do we determine our own behavior? What rules are written down and followed or ignored? What rules are not recorded but enforced? Where and how can we learn that a behavior is not "against the rules" but is still not culturally acceptable?

Every culture structures norms for each of these categories of activity. Each culture can be described by how these activities are recognized and valued.

- What are the boundaries in your culture?
- Who can do each activity?
- Who is not expected to do it?
- Who is prohibited and who isn't?
- Under what conditions?
- What happens when someone is outside the boundaries of the norm?
- How should we feel about someone ignoring the norm or advocating a different norm?

Teachers often think of their school as an institution or bureaucracy that rarely changes, rather than as a community with a culture that changes over time. The process of analyzing a school as a culture can help teachers understand about the activities that are shared with other cultures and those that are different from cultures outside the school. The real questions begin when teachers consider not just these activities but their norms and how they came to be. Then, they can think about how these cultural norms and activities can be changed by people who are part of the school culture.

The five CREED categories of activities can be used as lenses to view the culture of your school or community to understand it as an anthropologist might. For example, compare the culture in your school with the culture in your community. First, consider the creative activities in your school and community cultures:

- What are creative activities?
- Who does them?
- Where and when are they done?
- How are they accepted and valued?

Second, identify the representative artifacts of your school and community cultures:

- What do you typically find in your school classrooms or in the homes of your community?
- What things are the same and what are different?
- Why do they look, feel, and function in a particular way?

Third, decide what the emotive activities are in your school and community cultures:

- Where do they happen?
- Who is involved?
- What are the norms for behavior?
- How do you account for the differences?

Fourth, determine the evaluative activities in your school and community cultures:

- What do grades indicate?
- What are the norms for assessment in your school?
- Do people use narrative reports, portfolios, or conferences with parents?
- Are people graded in the community?
- How are they evaluated and by whom?

Fifth, think about how rules are made in your school and community cultures:

- Is there a democratic process involved?
- How are the rules announced and displayed?
- Who enforces the rules?
- Are the same rules applied to everyone or are they selective?
- What happens if you violate them?
- Do the same norms apply in the community as in the school?

MAKING SENSE OF CULTURE
IN LEARNING CIRCLES

The learning circle, within or outside a community of learners, provides a safe place for professionals to come to a deeper understanding of individual and group cultural assumptions. The organizational culture of a workplace may be uncomfortable or limiting for some members. Others may feel it is socially uncomfortable or taboo to raise issues of ethnic or racial cultural realities in a society as diverse as the United States. We may not know how to go about recognizing and changing our own work or community culture in positive ways. We may not agree on what is a "positive" change. We may not know how to identify traits in someone else's culture or, worse, may identify another culture as substandard compared with our own simply because it is different from our own. Our culture itself may not support developing awareness of cultural similarities and differences. As the world becomes smaller through technology, more and more cultures come into contact with each other on a regular basis and the potential for cultural conflicts and misunderstandings increases. Yet, there are very few "safe" venues for learning how to understand and communicate productively across cultural differences.

A learning circle can provide a "time-out," a safe place to experiment and to identify ways in which the larger culture may support or limit learning. The learning circle can also be a place where members agree to change some of the basic assumptions about the relationships between teachers, learners, and knowledge, thereby creating and experiencing a new culture that is more supportive than the culture surrounding the circle. It is a place where members can con-

sider and identify techniques for changing the larger culture of a
school or community in positive ways. Mike reported at the end of
his 2-year program:

> I experience changing cultures on a daily level in my classroom.
> Each year, the children seem different from the year before.
> Teachers need to change their teaching to fit the needs of cultures
> as they change. Teachers need to build communities within their
> classrooms and extend the boundaries of those communities to
> include families, friends, and neighbors. Teachers need to pro-
> vide support for learning and change. I learned how to do this in
> a more thoughtful fashion in my program.

Most professional development programs intended to transform
cultures are not as proactive in design and implementation as the Concordia Language Villages. Most professionals do not have the luxury
of sustaining an uninterrupted community over time and across
multiple learning events. In fact, most learning is tucked here and there
between other ongoing demands of families, jobs, exercise, or leisure.
But even a loosely defined membership under less-than-supportive
learning conditions can study its own culture and can deliberately
constitute and sustain a community that supports learning and its
membership. Here, we approach cultural transformation from three
levels of engagement: as learners, mentors, and leaders. In the next
sections, we offer examples of how learners might approach understanding culture through artifacts, dance, and script readings.

LEARNING ABOUT CULTURES THROUGH ARTIFACTS

Exploring cultural differences with different physical objects is a
fun, engaging, yet stretching, way to learn. Here is an example that
each of us has used in different variations. At the first session, participants are grouped in teams of four and are presented with an
artifact that most will not know. This can be a unique cooking, car-
pentry, or medical tool. We have used wooden artifacts that are variations of a carpenter's tool from 19th-century Korea. We have used
"things that can clean ears." We have used colored spindles from a
woolen mill in Wales.

Development of this activity started with a beautifully carved wooden ear cleaner from Japan, which the rest of us could not identify. Even with a clue about which culture it came from and what kind of store it could be purchased in, we still were not able to identify the function. When we learned what it was, we quickly realized that our ability to determine the function was limited by the fact that we equated cotton swab with "ear cleaning." We then discovered that a crochet hook looked more like the Japanese artifact than did a cotton swab. We began to collect "things that look like a long-handled, small-bowled spoon" from local hardware and cooking stores and soon had a set of artifacts that could be classified in many ways during the analysis of possible function.

You can look for dissimilar artifacts as well as ones that look alike but have different functions. A quick trip to a hardware store, a sporting goods store, a surplus store, a craft store, or a sewing store can yield an inexpensive supply of artifacts related to different kinds of activities so it is unlikely that any one person in the learning circle will know what everything is. On the other hand, it is likely that someone in any group of more than 10 people will know the use for any particular artifact. If you really want to make sure that there is something that no one is likely to identify, throw in something from a distant culture or historical time. Or put something in the collection such as a carved piece of wood that has no function other than its existence as art.

There are several ways to use artifacts as a successful learning tool. The following description explains a generic process for examining unknown cultural artifacts:

1. Think about how human beings approach something new (an object, person, concept, or culture). What do you do? How do you feel?

2. How do you handle this artifact? Perhaps you could draw it or write about your sensory experience of it.

3. Reflect in a journal on your present physical experience with the artifact, as well as prior knowledge and similar images that may occur during reflection.

4. Use these reflections to dialogue with a colleague about what you have learned about the artifact and your process of approaching something new. Speculate together and make one

or two logical inferences about what the artifact might be. Did you learn anything more about the artifact by sharing individual observations?

5. Generate questions you can reasonably answer from your inquiry thus far and questions that will give you more information.

6. Decide together about a possible context for this artifact. Where might it be used: in a kitchen, a workshop, a church, or a bath?

7. Try to name the artifact and speculate on a corresponding object in your culture.

8. Have the person who introduced the artifact name it and describe the cultural context. Then revisit the artifact and reconstruct how it works.

From this perspective the whole learning circle can then discuss the psychology, culture, and pedagogy of using artifacts and inquiry.

LEARNING ABOUT CULTURES
THROUGH DANCE

In a similar manner, it is possible to use movement or actions instead of artifacts, as we suggest in this second example. Walter recently participated in a dance activity that was not only a lived experience of learning but also fun and a real eye-opener for him, a self-declared "nondancer!" A group of 30 K-12 teachers was gathered together for a week around the topic, "Creating a Civic Culture in Schools and Classrooms." Each member brought to his or her learning circle within this community of learners something that he or she thought could enhance community building in a school. Denise, a vivacious elementary music teacher, and her husband, Tom, spent 3 hours the evening before the class creating a dance routine/pattern to popular American music. They invented a learning sequence so the group could learn experientially together and took the whole group through a dance learning experience. Walter said about his experience:

We practiced the steps together. I don't usually see myself as a dancer, but perhaps since I had spent all week with these colleagues building and exploring community, I had a deep sense of trust and well-being. I could be a 48-year-old dancer who had not danced publicly in 20 years. Like everyone else, I got so involved in learning the complicated moves and spins that I didn't think about how I was learning or about how I might look. After just 10 minutes of "practice," we danced 4 minutes to the music. Me, too! I was dancing! I didn't think about how I was learning or how Denise taught. I just learned, and danced, and had a great time.

Denise described what she was doing as "a community of dancers dancing in community." She was a colleague, collaborator, and consultant to active learning. The community and each individual in the community could reflect after the activity from different points of view about her "teaching" and individual and group "learning." When the group had finished the formal dance part of the exercise, everyone took several minutes to reflect in journals. Walter described a number of interconnections and perspectives:

I had a strong sense of how *in dance* I could assume the multiple roles of artisan, citizen, theologian, and scholar and the insights therefrom. By dancing, we are assuming roles of action (artisan, or citizen actor, for example) in which we are embedded in a particular context or scene with a script or pattern of acting meaningfully, which we can then, "after the dance," be scholarly about as we feel and think about significance.

Other action activities can be drawn from making music, singing, drumming, handicrafts, clapping games, juggling, or acting. The third example offers another way to engage learners in understanding their own perspectives on learning, culture, and transformation.

LEARNING ABOUT CULTURES THROUGH ACTING

Diane has used a piece of film script from Marguerite Duras's *Hiroshima Mon Amour* (1961) to explore different ways of learning about cultural differences. She has participants in communities of learners assume the roles of characters in the stories. Most people do not think of themselves as "actors," even though they may be "on stage" in their classroom 5 days a week. Many people are very shy about "playing a role" and may be worried about the need to memorize lines or "act." But use of a "reader's theater" format with the script always available in the reader's hand and describing what is going to happen as "reading a story to each other" instead of as "acting" makes many fears drop away quickly. Different small groups are assigned different pieces of the story and practice reading their piece quietly and then aloud to each other. Then, the "play" is staged. It is important in this activity to move quickly from each practice step to the "performance" so that no one has time to reflect during the activity. It is also important to introduce the whole activity as "just a different way" of presenting text for discussion and not as a "play."

A very powerful effect can be achieved in even 10 or 15 minutes of familiarization with the script, followed quickly by the reading. This particular play has proven rich in ways to explore cultural assumptions about history, culture, love, war, and human inhumanity to other humans. Because there are American, Japanese, French, and German aspects to the play, it can open discussion about different cultures. Written reflections after the reading and after the discussion of the reading can include prompts about learning as well as about cultural assumptions. A film or television program appropriate to participants' age and learning level can be used instead of the Duras piece. Diane has used an excerpt on secrets from the film *Dead Poets Society* with middle school students and an excerpt on Belle's love of books from the film *Beauty and the Beast* with 12-year-old girls and boys. She has used the topics of gender assumptions and age expectations as prompts for reflection about cultural differences.

These three examples offer ways of knowing about culture, our own and others. By participating in such learning, we are able to see our culture and others' cultures in different ways. In the next section, we explore ways that mentorship in schools helps transform cultures.

MENTORING OTHERS ABOUT CULTURE

The learning circle builds on our earliest understanding about how people learn—through *mentorship*. Most of us hear the term mentorship and imagine a one-on-one relationship of two people, one more mature and experienced than the other. The learning circle offers possibilities of "group mentorship," where several people work closely together for the good of the newest members and each other. Thoughtful professional development models use the concept of group mentorship, recognizing that one or two individuals cannot grow and learn as successfully outside the community of the department or school (Harris & Collay, 1990).

In the culture of a school, mentors are usually experienced teachers who agree to enculturate new members into the community and the profession. School cultures are complex and replete with spoken and unspoken customs, traditions, and norms whereby enculturation occurs whether these are articulated or not. Formal efforts to describe these customs, traditions, and norms by senior teachers contribute directly to the development of a healthy professional culture rather than leaving them unspoken to baffle the newest members of the profession.

Mentors also play a critical role in transforming an organization:

1. Mentors must be competent and qualified in their own right, having learned the lessons and participated in the kinds of cultural transmissions described above. In their role as mentors, they are carriers of the school culture.

2. Mentors accept responsibility for that culture; rather than standing back and claiming no relationship to the workings of the building, they take ownership of their role in creating the organization.

3. Mentors identify ways they can formally and informally structure the learning of new members and experienced colleagues. As full members of the community, their role is clear. They are responsible for structuring their learning and the learning of newcomers, creating a culture of support and growth in their school.

Mentors can play a key role in organizing learning circles within a school or district. They can convene colleagues in small groups for professional development and include newcomers in these gatherings. They can put their energy into group mentorship not only to transmit the culture of their organization but also to transform that culture by studying it and suggesting ways to make positive changes.

An example of a team of mentors who changed the culture of their school is a learning circle of four experienced teachers in an urban elementary school. These teachers found that students who were not labeled deficient but were not thriving seemed to be falling through the cracks. This team wrote a grant to hire and train paraprofessionals to work one-on-one with students they identified as "needing adult attention." The teachers created training materials for the paraprofessionals and designed curriculum materials for the students focusing on tutoring in reading and mathematics.

The team invited teacher colleagues to send any students they felt needed extra adult attention. The students did not need to meet specific criteria but did need their teacher's recommendation. About five or six children from each classroom attended these special support sessions throughout the year, and they all showed measurable improvement in attendance and in the quality of their work. The team received overwhelming praise from the faculty, the administration, and the district, and members are working to lever the project into other schools.

CULTURAL ASSUMPTIONS ABOUT LEADERS

In Western cultures, leadership is typically defined as those qualities that allow an individual to get other people to do things that are desirable, valued, or identified as goals. Leaders are similarly defined as people who have "leadership" traits or abilities and are in a leadership role. Humans have been arguing over and experimenting with how leaders can be identified and picked for as long as there have been oral and written traditions. We have also not agreed on the definitions for the same length of time!

Leadership in schools reflects many of the same conditions that are limiting progress in mainstream culture. For instance, the majority of teachers are women, and the majority of formal leaders are men. In districts where a majority of students are of color, the majority of teachers are white. Surely, there are capable leaders among these groups that are underrepresented. In addition to capacity building for individuals, organizations must build capacity by expanding their ranks to include leaders of both genders and all races. Organizations must also expand notions of what it means to lead, taking lessons from women and minorities who offer alternative ways of leading derived from their own experiences (Dunlap & Schmuck, 1995). Many teachers recognize this cultural challenge as well. Kevin described his learning in this way:

> This program has provided a forum for discussing issues related to culture. Our [group] has had time to get to know each other and we have seen the diversity within our own group. This diversity enhanced our group discussions and broadened our perceptions. There were many ways which we gained appreciation for other cultures, such as drumming, art, reading, and special speakers. We valued the opportunity to broaden our perception of the world and those who inhabit it. As educators, we feel a responsibility to provide opportunities for our students that broaden their perspectives. This aspect of our learning has affirmed this in us and inspired us to continue to help children look beyond their own experiences.

The word leadership implies that there must be followers to be a leader or leaders. The concept is relational in nature. Successful leadership is determined by many things: Someone thinks or agrees that one or more people are leaders; the leader(s) also agrees and acts as the leader; and the actions lead to positive results in an organizational or political context and at a particular time and place—as determined at the time *and* as determined on historical reflection. It is not possible to define a leader separate from the time, place, events, organization, and other people involved both during and following the leadership events.

In other words, concepts of leadership are culturally bound. Thus, activities that make explicit individual and group assumptions about appropriate leadership in the learning circle also provide an excellent ground for discussions of cultural differences. One method that we have each used successfully in multiple settings is to have the group pick a metaphor for what the learning circle is currently or what they hope it could be. Individuals can be asked to create a metaphor and describe why they chose it by writing a brief paragraph, drawing a picture, or creating a collage. Then, all the metaphors can be shared with the learning circle.

Each of these metaphors contains assumptions about leaders and followers. The learning circle should think about the implicit assumptions in their metaphorical examples and what a good leader should do and should *not* do. Describe an organization or community that is opposite in character of the learning circle. What does leadership looks like in this "bad" organization? This will give the learning circle something with which to contrast "good" group behaviors. Once a list of "good" and "bad" leadership behaviors is completed, decide if these behaviors are *always* the best ones.

If the learning circle has selected collaboration, consensus, or democratic voting as always being the best, then what about unusual conditions such as a fire in the building or a bomb threat? If the group has selected a democratically elected leader, then what kinds of things should the leader do to make sure he or she always expresses the desire of the majority? Is serving the majority what the leader should do? Should minorities ever be served, or should the leader follow personal ethics or beliefs when they differ from the majority? Through this kind of discussion, a typical learning circle will decide that leadership differs for every time and place. Another variation on this activity is to discuss what leadership or power relationships are embedded in the typical teacher-student relationship. Can power ever be equal in either situation? Can collaboration or democracy coexist when power relations are never equal?

Another discussion that will quickly surface individual definitions and norms, as well as cultural assumptions about the relationship of the individual to the group, is one on leadership:

- Do learning circle members believe that "leaders are made, not born"?
- Do they believe that leadership is a shared aspect of the learning circle or that only some people are leaders?
- Do they believe that it is a good thing to designate one person as the learning circle leader?
- Do they believe that leadership should be permanent or rotated or shared?
- Does everyone have a vote?

Most learning circles experience some movement of leadership between the members, depending on topic and activity. Discussing how personal concepts of individual leadership skills change over time is a good periodic cultural review activity.

Any of these examples can lead back to a review of the learning circle covenant and how leaders and leadership behaviors are defined, encouraged, and discouraged by the covenant. Any of these discussions can also lead to discussion of how leader selection and behavior may differ

1. Within a learning circle
2. Within a community of learners or individual classrooms
3. Within the surrounding culture of the sponsoring school or university
4. Within the broader community in which the members are located or in other organizations to which the members belong
5. Within the larger state or nation
6. Compared with other countries

This layered analysis can be used to identify when and where appropriate leadership exists, where it does not exist, where it is encouraged, and where it is punished. Resulting discussion is quite revealing about how hard it can be to create and sustain a relatively safe place in which to explore and become good at leadership behaviors that support learning. It can also provide a sobering and realistic view of how difficult it may be to change surrounding cultures.

TEACHING AS LEADING

The construction of such a shared meaning culture with defined roles is a developmental process. Senge and Kim (1997) argue, "Human communities have always attempted to organize themselves to maximize the production, transmittal and application of knowledge. People are called upon to play the roles of elders, doers, and coaches or teachers" (p. 2). They maintain that in these activities different individuals fulfill different roles with varying degrees of success. Three activities that they term "theory building, practices, and capacity building are interconnected and interwoven as the primary fabric of the community, in a seamless process that restores and advances the knowledge of the [group]" (p. x).

Over time, members grow in leadership by sharing ownership and responsibilities in the learning circle. Of course, their growth and the evolution of the larger community depend on a variety of factors. At the heart of a learning circle's capacity for authentic equity and justice in relationships is the leadership of the facilitators and the interests and commitments of a critical mass of shareholders. Deliberately structured experiences by community leaders provide opportunities for members to gain the insights and skills needed to be full participants in a democratic society.

We can think of the issue in terms of whole-to-part power relationships between individuals and society with the domination of the relationship by the whole (society, community) or by parts (rugged individualism). Typical forms of whole-to-part relations are school communities that are either principal-directed or teacher-centered and classrooms that are teacher-directed or student-centered. Both situations create a lack of reciprocity between the members, and the authority and power relationships remain limited by traditional notions of authority and power. On the other hand, an interactive holism of individual and group is a cooperative union of shared responsibilities based on a respectful mutuality of common ground or a compact of reciprocity. Out of this social context arises roles of citizenship and leadership. Esmerelda described her experience in a graduate program organized around a community of learners:

> From the beginning, our facilitators made it obvious that they were there to support our learning. We were given the freedom to do what was most beneficial to our learning, without many boundaries. We found that we were more enthused about our projects and did a quality job without explicit, mandated directions. We experienced excellent role models in [supporting] learning. They compelled us to make adjustments in our practice that allowed our students as much freedom as possible.

Perhaps the most significant picture of leadership, however, is the modeling done by the leaders in our graduate program. The behaviors of people who lead a community of learners can be used as a meta-teaching activity focused on culture and leadership. Cathy describes what leaders teach by the ways they lead:

> The method used to support the students' learning was one of facilitator rather than director. Responsibility was always handed back to the learner. No "answers" were ever provided. There was not a "right way" to do things. I had been very successful in the past as a traditional student. I could take notes and

spit it back out with the best of them. I was quite skilled at determining what the teacher wanted and giving them exactly that. The experience of having my learning supported through a constructivist approach was terrifying, frustrating, and challenging. It was the first time in my academic life that I ever considered that I might not be adequate to the task. . . . The result of 2 years of living with this . . . is that . . . [I have] changed my relationship to learning and to myself in a fundamental way. I did not realize prior to this that I had not taken responsibility for my learning, that I approached learning with an external focus of authority, that it had been a dance of compliance and resistance. I now take full responsibility for my own learning. I learned this from [my leaders].

We believe that leadership, like followership and learning, is resident in the whole group as well as in individuals. We believe that many different forms of leadership may serve learning well at different times, and that the way a learning circle determines what works best at a particular time is by reviewing how the six conditions are applied. The concept that leadership exists as a group trait rather than an individual trait is initially difficult for many teachers to grasp. The activities we described allow expansion of embedded concepts of leadership in a nonthreatening and developmental manner. Here is what Rosalie said about her sense of culture and leadership after going through these activities in her learning circle:

In dealing with such a changing society in regard to cultures, races, and values, I have found myself doing more group work in order to establish more of a sense of community in my room, more cooperation among the children, and a more general sense for everyone about the roles that I play in supporting the children's learning.

FOR FURTHER READING

Morgan, G. (1989). *Creative organization theory: A resource book.* Newbury Park, CA: Sage.

Wheatley, M. (1992). *Leadership and the new science.* San Francisco: Berrett-Koehler.

CHAPTER EIGHT

RE-CREATING CONDITIONS

Thematic investigation [circles] thus becomes a common striving towards awareness of reality and towards self-awareness, which makes this investigation a starting point for the educational process or for cultural action of a liberating character.

Paulo Freire
(1970, p. 98)

As teachers become involved in learning circles, we expect them to move toward awareness of themselves and of the reality of the schools and communities where they work. As Paulo Freire (1970) might have expected from his "culture circles," we would expect that learning circles of teachers would become a starting point for education or action that would liberate them. This certainly was true for our learning circle of coauthors as we re-created the conditions we had previously experienced in many other healthy communities of learners. We consciously incorporated the six essential conditions we were writing about to put our thinking into practice. We were building community by repeating rituals of reconnecting our personal lives and sharing food and laughter. We were constructing knowledge for ourselves by starting with our own language and thinking as a basis for our writing. We were supporting learners by actively listening to one another, giving positive feedback, and encouraging critique. We were documenting reflection by writing and revising drafts of stepping-stones, stories, and chapters. We were assessing expectations by collecting drafts of our work, selecting pieces to be included, reflecting on edits and suggestions for improvement, and inspecting each other's chapters. Finally, we were changing cultures by the influence and impact that our work together was having on our respective positions and workplaces.

Michelle, as lead author, reflected on the re-creation of our authors' learning circle:

> When we started this project, we were all involved as faculty at one institution. Our experiences as leaders of communities of learners and coordinators of learning circles were from all over this country, Canada, and Japan. Over the 3 years we thought together and worked on this book, there have been many changes in our small circle. Diane has left higher education but uses her skills as a facilitator in her church community; George is now an educational consultant and a facilitator for another learning community program; and Walter continues to work with professional development in schools, where he uses learning circles in a very deliberate way. I have stepped away from my work with faculty development in higher education to write, think, and be a new mother at midlife.
>
> The nature of our learning circles reflects the six conditions we have endeavored to re-create for ourselves, and we know that they have been central to our success as adult learners in transition. Our academic work might proceed without attention to these conditions, but our personal and professional development would not. The quality of our own professional development is key to our thinking about the profession of teaching. In our next learning circle, we expect to excuse some and invite others to join us. The newly organized learning circle will retain some landmarks of this group, yet move into new terrain. We look forward to the next leg of the journey.

The most important application of the learning circle experience is the opportunity for teachers to re-create the conditions for other communities of learners in classrooms, schools, or districts. Re-creating these conditions involves reweaving the six essential conditions of learning circles into a tapestry on another loom. As teachers experience these conditions for themselves, they should be able to reproduce these important conditions for other groups of teachers or students. The most important places for re-creating these conditions are the classrooms, schools, or districts where teachers work every day.

How do teachers use the six essential conditions for healthy communities of learners in this book? Individual teachers need ways to move beyond talk and into action. One teacher with a good idea can seek involvement from other teachers, members of the staff, and parents. Some of our teachers have moved toward re-creating communities of learners in their classrooms, whereas others have re-created learning circles in their grade-level teams, school buildings, districts, or cities. Teacher leaders have created paraprofessional training materials to improve their partnerships with colleagues who have support roles in the school. Other teacher leaders have moved their site councils to function more as a community of learners. Some teachers have their students adopt a service learning project in which they interview senior citizens at their residences and write up their biographies and learn a great deal about the history of their community and heritage of its residents. Other teachers involve their students in learning teams to produce HyperStudio presentations of their cultural heritage. Teachers from different schools meet to create alternative assessment procedures for mathematics and then try to adapt them to their own classrooms. Some of these examples began with a single person with a good idea; some grew from a grade-level team with a fine arts or environmental education grant; others started with teachers sharing a topic of interest in their school or district. All of these are examples of using the six essential conditions for healthy communities of learners in one's own practice.

RECONSTRUCTING LEARNING CIRCLES

We urge teachers to focus on forming a learning circle with a few colleagues to create opportunities for their own professional development that incorporate all six conditions of healthy communities of learners. They should be able to identify some examples from their own experiences in education or organizations or corporations that qualify as prototypes for them to use in creating these conditions:

- Were there times when you were involved in a group that exhibited some of these conditions?

- When were you involved in **building community** between members of an organization as part of their coming together rather than leaving it to outside influences or informal socializing?
- When do you remember trying to engage in **constructing knowledge** with others rather than just adopting the opinions or vocabulary of "experts"?
- Did you ever participate in a group that was **supporting learners** by encouraging them to talk about what they were constructing and thinking as they learned?
- Were there times when members of a class kept journals or made entries in electronic conference areas individually and then shared them regularly with the others for the purpose of **documenting reflection** beyond their personal use?
- Were you ever on a board that set its own learning agenda and then periodically took time for **assessing expectations** members had established for themselves and others to monitor their progress?
- When were you in a committee that set out to participate in **changing cultures** of its organization or community by raising questions about established policies or convenient routines that no longer seemed to benefit most members?

Examples of some of these conditions should be within your realm of experience.

Your challenge is to consolidate your memories of these experiences and to integrate the six conditions into a learning circle of colleagues who would participate in taking responsibility for their own professional development as a healthy community of learners. Many communities of learners exhibit some of these characteristics, but few are using the synergy created by these conditions as the six separate parts are combined into a dynamic whole that functions as a living organization by self-organizing, self-regulating, and adapting. Many of us have difficulty just keeping our own separate systems in concert to live a healthy life without the struggle to bring in several other professional colleagues who are wrestling with their own demons. The journey is usually easier if you don't make it alone, however, but have others to walk and talk and think with along the way! You form a traveling group like a bicycle tour when you decide together where you are going, each on his or her individual machine but going with one another, stopping along the way to share food and water and observations about the weather, landscape, and roadway. You record and share your individual thoughts with the tour group and constantly monitor your progress to your destination and each other's well-being.

PRACTICAL CONSIDERATIONS

One way to think about the reconstruction of learning circles to create conditions for your own professional development is to use the biological metaphor of a living organization. The three constant functions of a living organization, self-organization, self-regulation, and adaptation, can be applied to a learning circle as well as to individuals. The health of your community of learners is based on integrating the six conditions as we have described, but this vehicle for professional development also has movement over time. **Initiating, maintaining, sustaining,** and **transforming** the learning circle are important periods in the cycle of growth.

Initiating involves convening the group for the first time and answering several questions:

- Who do you want to invite to join with you?
- When will you meet?
- Where will you gather?
- What will be your purpose?
- How will you represent the idea and conditions of a learning circle?

All of these need to be addressed before you call a meeting and have some other teachers show up. We recommend thinking these things through with others who might want to be involved and working together to set up an initial gathering with an agenda that will be configured at that time, rather than one person trying to do all the front-end work and being looked to as the leader of the group. The more the responsibility is shared, the more ownership all the participants will feel.

The **maintaining** tasks should be considered by the group at the initial meeting and again involve several questions:

- Would you like to invite other people to join your learning circle? We have seen them function with three to eight people, but five or six seem optimal.
- When could you gather on a regular basis?
- Where will you meet?
- What agreements do you need to make about membership, keeping on schedule, bringing refreshments, and making decisions?

We have scheduled ourselves to meet almost every week by keeping the same time available and usually planning on meeting in the same place until that needs to change. Often, not everyone can be there, but those who can still benefit. Weekly may be too frequent for some, but monthly is usually not enough to feel movement. Perhaps, every 2 or 3 weeks would work. Saturday morning breakfast at a restaurant is one way to accommodate people from different schools and districts. Monday night at a coffee house might give you something to look forward to at the start of the week, except for football fans. We know many teachers who prefer to gather on Tuesday or Thursday after school when they don't have faculty meetings. Wednesday is church night for many, and Friday is usually too much to ask. Sunday evening might be another time to get together conveniently as the weekend winds down. This is the kind of decision that the group might make at the first meeting; we encourage you to use a consensus approach and make sure everyone's voice is heard and agrees with the others. Learning circles are for personal and professional development not for institutional management!

The **sustaining** tasks involve more long-term nurturing and care for the group:

- What rituals are important to your learning circle?
- Do you have opening or closing ceremonies?
- What do people want to learn or to do?
- What kinds of support do different learners need?
- What expectations does each member have?

- What larger environments have an impact on your learning circle?
- Will you keep journals, develop portfolios, or regularly share your reflections in writing?

These are perhaps the keys to a healthy community of learners. We usually begin each session with a time to catch up on each other's personal lives: minor crises, family catastrophes, professional victories, personal obstacles, or general reflections about goings-on since we last got together. This provides us an opportunity to take the emotional temperature of the group and look at each other again as changed beings. The key decisions are usually around a common project or projects related to a common theme that gives some focus to the regular interactions so everyone has a sense of participating in his or her own learning but sharing in the spirit of the circle as a colleague among equals. Individuals take on different roles and tasks in the group. Some are brainstormers, some are doers, some are talkers, some are listeners, some are writers, some are editors, some are readers, some are thinkers, some are organizers, some are managers, but everyone has a role that affects the others in the learning circle, and each role must become visible and considered by the group. Implicit in these considerations is that you are truly creating conditions for teacher professional development among those involved in the learning circle. You are building community, constructing knowledge, supporting learners, documenting reflection, assessing expectations, and changing cultures as you think together to answer the questions we posed.

Transforming usually comes at a time when most learning circles must come to some closing. People move away, others want to join, the project gets completed, or the logistics become too complicated to continue. At these times it is important to acknowledge the transformation of the learning circle, the completion of a never-ending ring like the passage of 12 hours on a clock that represents the movement of time but not an end. Many learning circles will continue as a spiral on another level with different participants for most involved. Others will just dissolve for the participants until they find such conditions again. This should be cause for celebration and joy for the end of one journey together and the beginning of another with different traveling companions. We encourage you to take some time to reflect on this closing and honor the journey with respect for fellow travelers. We often drift or sneak away from groups without stopping to sing the last refrain together and celebrate the completion of a journey that we have taken with others before moving on to the next adventure. Don't go away without saying good-bye. Take time to appreciate each other and your time together by arranging for a closing to the learning circle.

Perhaps, the best way to develop a healthy community of learners is to not focus separately on each of the six conditions but to be involved in a common task that focuses the collective energies of those involved on creating something themselves: an answer to a question, a solution to a problem, a metaphor to make an explanation, or a goal to set a standard. Being involved with a group of "collaborative learners" in the process of making meaning as they care for one another and record their thinking about evaluating their processes or products and impacting their cultural setting is a seamless approach to using these six conditions as the woof for the warp of a particular project that becomes the tapestry woven by all participants in a learning circle.

VARIATIONS ON A THEME

Communities of learners are made up of several variations on the theme of learning circles. This would include learning circles composed of teachers at one grade level in an elementary school; teachers from different disciplines in a secondary school; teachers who include a principal, parent, and aide in their group; teachers who include interns, subs, and student teachers in their gatherings; teachers who come together from preschool, primary, intermediate, middle, and senior high levels; or teachers who invite business partners, school board members, and teacher educators to join them in their get-togethers. Such examples are diagrammed in the Learning Circles Schematic in Figure 8.1.

There is no set configuration for a learning circle, but we encourage teachers to invite others interested in education to become part of their professional development group and to share in a reciprocal process of review, feedback, and change that accompanies their ongoing learning about teaching and makes their efforts more visible to the school and community. Our intent is not to define all the possibilities for forming learning circles but rather to show that there are many different ways of including others in a collaborative process of professional development.

Learning Circles Schematic

Figure 8.1. Learning Circles Schematic

The idea of learning circles is adapted from several precedents. We continue to grow in our understanding of communities of learners both through our lived experience as learners and teachers and through a dialogue with others who share a similar perspective. Emphasis on group work, teaming, and cooperative groups or "circles of learning" (Johnson & Johnson, 1986) are increasingly prevalent in educational settings, as are teaming and "quality circles" (Deming, 1986) in business. The Holmes Group (1990) has strongly advocated for "learning communities" in teacher education and professional development. Barbara Rogoff and her associates (Rogoff, Matusov, & White, 1996) write about the roles of participants in "sharing circles" for early childhood education that are neither teacher nor student centered but based on a reciprocal responsibility between teacher and student. "Study circles" were prevalent in the settlement houses, factories, and libraries of early 20th-century America as informal and practical methods for adult education and social change. These sound very similar in purpose to the "culture circles" or "the-

Table 8.1 Correspondence Between Elements and Conditions

Design Element	Essential Condition
Situation	Changing Cultures
Groupings	Building Community
Bridge	Constructing Knowledge
Questions	Supporting Learners
Exhibit	Assessing Expectations
Reflections	Documenting Reflections

matic investigation circles" advocated for critical thinking by Freire (1970). The World School for Adventure Learning pioneered the idea of on-line "project circles" for students from different schools around the world who were working on similar projects involving water quality in lakes or rivers, arctic ecosystems, or wildlife impact.

These precursors have laid a solid foundation on which to build our current framework for professional development of teachers and other independent learners. We have even tried to coordinate our constructivist learning design with the six essential conditions for healthy communities of learners. We believe that this demonstrates how the six conditions can be incorporated in a classroom learning event of even a short time frame. The Correspondence Between Elements and Conditions in Table 8.1 shows how one maps into the other. The order of the design does not match the order of the conditions as we have presented them. We have discussed the importance of integrating and weaving all six conditions into a whole fabric of experience, however. We see threads of each condition as the woof of our constructivist learning design and the warp as the particular situation that is chosen for explanation. Exploring this relationship was one of the last exercises to "walk our talk" that we engaged in as a learning circle of coauthors.

RE-CREATING CONDITIONS IN CLASSROOMS

Students will benefit from your experience with a learning circle as you focus on your own professional development, but you can also apply some of the same processes by re-creating conditions for learning circles in your classroom. Students can see themselves as members of communities of learners if some of the same conditions are part of their classroom experience. Learning circles are a good forum for student support, reflection, and assessment. Accountability for such things as citizenship, scholarship, artisanship, learning, journals, portfolios, and behavior can all become a part of learning circle expectations. Students can often hold one another to a higher standard than adults would expect. Like adults, kids can benefit from working in small groups by

- Building community as part of a team
- Constructing knowledge as they decide what they want to do and how to do it
- Supporting learners in their group
- Documenting reflection through journals, graphic displays, or multimedia presentations
- Assessing expectations by making decisions together about what they want to do and how they will evaluate what they have done
- Changing cultures in their classroom, school, or community

Students can work on class or school projects together as teams within a larger group. Service learning projects with a focus on the larger community where they live are positive ways to engage students with their environment. Apprenticeships are another wonderful opportunity for them to experience the adult world of work and interaction apart from the academic curriculum of schools. Environmental education projects, including water quality investigations, traffic studies, or urban planning, offer ways to involve students in real-life inquiry about community problem solving.

A marvelous place for these learning circles of students to work is in their community. They could first survey the community to determine what the needs and priorities might be for a service learning program, apprenticeship arrangement, or environmental education project. Then, the class could decide what project to take on and involve their learning circles in working on a part of the project, such as publicity, volunteers, fund-raising, background information, and other tasks needing to be done. This kind of project builds positive relations with the community and gives students an opportunity to apply their skills in reading, writing, mathematics, science, and social studies by interacting with real people in their community to carry out tasks that would truly benefit everyone involved. Possibilities include designing neighborhood gardens or playgrounds; setting up orienting courses in parks; stenciling reminders near storm drains about flow into rivers, lakes, or bays; surveys of speed or volume of traffic on neighborhood streets; water quality testing or small watershed cleanup in local creeks; involving neighborhood senior citizen centers in school-related activities such as tutoring or having students help local seniors with fall or spring cleaning; publishing directories of local social service or nonprofit agencies who solicit volunteers; arranging child care for mothers of young children who volunteer in the school; providing tutoring services for adult literacy programs.

Some teachers we admire involve students in their own class project every year. One runs a cafe for 2 days, including planning the menus, buying the food, cooking and waiting tables for their families and other patrons, and donating the profits for a worthy cause. Another has her students focus on a theme of "Peace and Justice." They have chosen to fold paper cranes for Hiroshima victims, honor survivors of the holocaust, or visit nursing homes once a week. Walter has several suggestions for such activities in his *Birds of Peace* handbook (Enloe, 1996). Another teacher has won national awards for her class projects, such as stenciling storm drains that flow into local lakes or studying traffic patterns on streets near the school and presenting recommendations to the city council about speed and noise abatement. Rural teachers have received EPA grants to buy equipment and test water quality in regional watersheds, restore wetlands parks, or study deformed frogs. Some of these teachers have involved their students in on-line project circles with other schools, an idea pioneered by the World School as sort of an electronic learning circle to compile and compare results of similar projects in a variety of schools throughout the world.

Many of these projects incorporate the six conditions essential for healthy communities of learners. Part of every school day or week can be spent in learning circles with activities designed to encourage the same six conditions. Team building, collaborative thinking, and decision-making exercises would promote **building community.** Identifying their own projects and proposing plans to carry them out would form a basis for them **constructing knowledge** on their own, rather than following a prescribed curriculum or text-book. As they struggled together with learning to do such projects, students would be **supporting learners** in their own learning circle and learning to value positive relationships and reciprocity in giving and receiving support. By writing about their work and displaying it in journals, newsletters, or web pages, they are not only thinking about what they are doing but also **documenting reflection** and making it visible and available to others. As they make choices about what they will do, how they will do it, and how they will evaluate what they have done, they are **assessing expectations** they have set and how well they have accomplished what they wanted to do. In the process, they are often **changing cultures,** having a significant impact on their community by being a positive influence and pro-moting the common welfare of their fellow citizens through youth involvement rather than alienation.

The key again is working in learning circles or groups of about six students who meet regularly during these daily or weekly peri-ods and work together on their own agenda for personal growth as individuals in a nurturing group. Some students may want to ex-clude others from their group. Others may not want to be part of such a formal structure. These situations provide opportunities to ask the hard questions about the role of an individual in our society and membership in a group that they find accepts them, supports them as learners, helps them think through problems, and values their participation. We would recommend that students be involved in deciding

- How the groups are formed
- How everyone in the class is involved
- How they treat each other
- When they meet
- What their projects are
- What they expect from their group and the class
- How they determine whether these expectations are met

It might be easier for the teacher to make all these arrangements and decisions, but the students would not benefit from the autonomy and responsibility of a learning circle where students are making these choices themselves.

RE-CREATING CONDITIONS
IN SCHOOLS OR DISTRICTS

Perhaps, the most important implications of learning circles are that the six essential conditions can be re-created in schools and districts as well as classrooms. This story is about a school district that changed its culture because individual teachers took the risk to change classroom practice. A middle school principal who was active as an adjunct faculty member for a local university invited that institution to offer a new, innovative graduate program in her district. She brought information, arranged space, and encouraged teachers to participate. During the time that program was under way, she moved to the central office to direct professional development activities. Meanwhile, several of the teachers from the program joined with another principal to open a new school in the district. These teachers created a learning circle at their new building, replicating the learning circle they established in their program. Several more teachers in the new school joined the next cohort in the graduate program and created their own learning circle in the program and in the building. There was now a critical mass in the new school.

One of the teachers had carried her applied research project about supportive professional development to the superintendent and told him about the graduate program based on creating communities of learners. The building principal and the central office leader also talked with the superintendent about the concept, and all worked to carry the idea of "learning community" to the rest of the district. The principals met and agreed to convene themselves as a community of learners. At this writing, there is strong support among many principals and the district leadership to adopt the concept of "learning community" for their vision statement. Several district teachers and administrators are actively involved as faculty members at the university, completing the circle of knowledge sharing. In this way, teachers become true members of a democratic society where all voices are heard and each member is a contributor.

We realize that reform of education is a national agenda. It can proceed only from the bottom up, not the top down, however. Reform efforts are still being legislated on teachers by politicians and bureaucrats without teachers' commitment to change. There are new proposals for national tests in reading and math despite the improvements that new state and national standards have produced. The mayor has taken over operation of schools in Chicago, and schools in Washington, D.C., and elsewhere are no longer being run by elected boards of education and superintendents. These school boards were originally intended to hire and advise teachers for a single school with a few classrooms. The institutions of education have changed radically, with schools of hundreds or thousands of students and districts with tens of thousands of children in communities of hundreds of thousands and millions. The scale is so enormous that few board members or superintendents even know many of the teachers in larger districts. We propose that smaller communities of learners and more intimate learning circles of peers for professional development will help education return to its roots in community and democratic process. As students and teachers become involved with each other in communities of learners, we hope that they will see themselves as contributing members of their larger communities of city, state, nation, and world. Maybe, they will learn to value reading, math, and writing as access to their communities in this information age. Teachers can be prepared to lead them in this direction only if they have experienced communities of learners for themselves, or "been there, done that, got the t-shirt!" We expect that teacher leadership will have more impact on changing schools and districts from within. Most reform efforts have come up short because of resistance from within rather than lack of good intentions on the part of elected officials and administrators.

WHERE FROM HERE?

We really want teachers to belong to healthy communities of learners and take responsibility for their own professional development through learning circles. We need to give them some tools for diagnosing the health of their communities or circles and provide them with more resources for re-creating the six essential conditions for healthy communities of learners in their own learning circles. The Progress Toward Healthy Learning Circles in Table 8.2 summarizes the ideas and examples we have introduced in this book and ranks

Table 8.2 Progress Toward Healthy Learning Circles

Essential Condition	Phase I	Phase II	Phase III
Building Community	Rituals	Covenants	Processes
Constructing Knowledge	Questions	Thoughts	Descriptions
Supporting Learners	Listeners	Advocates	Reviewers
Documenting Reflection	Dialogues	Records	Journals
Assessing Expectations	Goals	Plans	Portfolios
Changing Cultures	Learners	Mentors	Leaders

them in developmental phases. This table should serve as a guide to where your community of learners or learning circle is currently on the spectrum of healthy development. It might also serve as a map for where you want to go. Each phase represents an integration of previous phases and a more complex elaboration of ideas and engagement with colleagues.

Building community begins with establishing **rituals** for opening, closing, and celebrating; continues with negotiating **covenants** around common values; and matures with organizing **processes** for decision making, problem solving, and well-being by the community. Constructing knowledge begins with individual and collective **questions;** continues with **thoughts** about answers through the symbolic systems of feelings, images, and languages; and matures as individuals present **descriptions** of their thinking for others to consider. Supporting learners begins as colleagues are respectful **listeners** to one another's stories, continues as they become **advocates** who encourage each other to grow, and matures when they accept one another as peer **reviewers.** Documenting reflection begins with **dialogues** about practice; continues with **records** of reflection through photos, tapes, or notes; and matures with excerpts from **journals** kept over time. Assessing expectations begins with agreeing on appropriate **goals** for all to accomplish; continues with making individual **plans** for growth toward accomplishing these goals; and matures with the collection, selection, reflection, and inspection of **portfolios** to show growth. Changing cultures begins with **learners** who apply the essential conditions in other settings and study the effects; continues with **mentors** who coach other teachers; and matures with teacher **leaders** who transform people, practice, and places.

We hope this description of developmental phases is useful for determining where you are and where you want to go. This book represents our first effort to describe our experiences and thoughts related to teacher professional development. We realize it is only an introduction and more resources are needed. Currently, other teachers are collaborating with us to prepare the *Handbook for Learning Circles,* which includes more ideas and exercises about creating conditions for teacher professional development. There has already been movement in education from administrators approving individual courses or credits for continuing education to "staff development committees" of teachers who approve professional development programs for peers. Learning circles represent the next step in the process of teachers taking responsibility for their own learning about development as professionals.

CONCLUSION

There is a rich and growing body of knowledge about learning available to educators and others who care about the intimate relationship between teaching and learning. We have cited several strands of theory and research that readers may wish to pursue as they seek greater understanding of the changes occurring in education. As a foundation for our thinking, we interwove six strands of theory that rely on the inventive, integrative, interdependent, and interactive images of learning by individuals in a complex adaptive system or a living organization that self-organizes, self-regulates, and adapts to its environment. We believe learning circles offer a model for professional development and personal transformation to school-based educators, university-based educators, and corporate trainers. This approach depends on teachers and others setting their own agenda for professional development by working with a small group of supportive colleagues in a learning circle to determine what they want to learn and how they will learn it. Learning and teaching are two sides of the same coin; the best teachers are lifelong learners. Teachers must make their own decisions and design experiences to further their own professional development agenda with respect, review, and reflection from caring collaborators. This is the heart of our thinking about creating conditions for teacher professional development in learning circles.

Stating a value for lifelong learning is an important first step, but it is not sufficient. The challenge is determining what philosophy and which values will generate practices that create conditions for adults and children to become lifelong learners. We encourage educators to create learning circles as intimate communities of learners for their own professional development and personal transformation of their practice. We are not alone. The National Board for Professional Teaching Standards has adopted this standard number five: "Teachers are members of learning communities" (NBPTS, 1991). The power of this forum for accomplishing the key conditions for professional development and personal transformation of practice is becoming widely recognized. We see it applying on the personal level to small groups of teachers who take responsibility for their own learning. They can weave the threads of their experience as teachers as a warp through the woof of the six essential conditions we have described: **building community, constructing knowledge, supporting learners, documenting reflection, assessing expectations,** and **changing cultures.** As these threads blend and bind together, the teachers create their own tapestry for others to see their craft and artistry!

REFERENCES

Bellah, R. N., Madsen, R., Sullivan, W. M., Swidler, A., & Tipton, S. M. (1991). *The good society.* New York: Vintage.

Bohm, D. (1981). *Wholeness and the implicate order.* London: Routledge & Kegan Paul.

Boyer, E. (1995). *The basic school: A community of learners.* Princeton, NJ: Carnegie Foundation for the Advancement of Teaching.

Brosterman, N. (1997). *Inventing kindergarten: Nineteenth-century children, twentieth-century art.* New York: Harry N. Abrams.

Bruner, J. (1996). *The culture of education.* Cambridge, MA: Harvard University Press.

Capra, F. (1996). *The web of life.* New York: Anchor.

Clandinin, D. J., Davies, A., Huber, J., Rose, C., & Whelan, K. (1997, April). *Narrative knowledge in teacher education.* Paper presented at the American Educational Research Association, Chicago.

Cooper, J., Collay, M., & Day, R. (1995, November). *Constructing the professional self through metaphor: Perspectives across three educational contexts.* Paper presented at the annual meeting of the Association for the Study of Higher Education, Orlando, FL.

Cooper, J., & Dunlap, D. (1991). Journal keeping for administrators. *Review of Higher Education, 15*(1), 65-82.

Csikszentmihalyi, M. (1990). *Flow: The psychology of optimal experience.* New York: Harper & Row.

D'Andrade, R. (1992). *Human motives and cultural models.* New York: Cambridge University Press.

Darling-Hammond, L. (1990). Teacher professionalism: Why and how. In A. Lieberman (Ed.), *Schools as collaborative cultures: Creating the future now* (pp. 25-50). New York: Falmer.

DeGeus, A. (1997). *The living company: Habits for survival in a turbulent business environment.* Boston, MA: Harvard Business School Press.

Deming, W. W. (1986). *Out of the crisis*. Cambridge: MIT Press.

Donaldson, M. (1996). Humanly possible: Education and the scope of the mind. In D. Olson & N. Torrance (Eds.), *The handbook of education and human development: New models of learning, teaching, and schooling.* Cambridge, MA: Blackwell.

Duckworth, E. (1987). *The having of wonderful ideas.* New York: Teachers College Press.

Dunlap, D., & Schmuck, P. (Eds.). (1995). *Women leading in education.* Albany: State University of New York Press.

Duras, M. (1961). *Hiroshima mon amour* (R. Seaver, Trans.). New York: Grove.

Enloe, W. (1996). *Birds of peace.* San Francisco: Whitewing.

Enloe, W., & Evans, K. (1996). *Creating context.* Tucson, AZ: Zephyr.

Flavell, J. (1963). *The developmental psychology of Jean Piaget.* Princeton, NJ: D. Van Nostrand.

Freire, P. (1970). *Pedagogy of the oppressed.* New York: Seabury.

Fullan, M. (1991). *The new meaning of educational change.* New York: Teachers College Press.

Furth, H. (1969). *Piaget and knowledge: Theoretical foundations.* Englewood Cliffs, NJ: Prentice Hall.

Gagnon, G., & Collay, M. (1996, June). *Constructivist learning design.* Paper presented at the 2nd Annual Qualitative Research Conference, St. Paul, MN.

Goodlad, J. (1984). *A place called school.* New York: McGraw-Hill.

Goodman, N. (1978). *Ways of worldmaking.* Indianapolis, IN: Hackett.

Greene, M. (1995). *Releasing the imagination: Essays on education, the arts, and social change.* San Francisco: Jossey-Bass.

Harris, M., & Collay, M. (1990). Teacher induction in rural schools. *Journal of Staff Development, 11*(4), 44-48.

Hollingsworth, S. (1994). *Teacher research and urban literacy education: Lessons and conversations in a feminist key.* New York: Teachers College Press.

Holmes Group. (1990). *Tomorrow's schools: Principles for the design of professional development schools.* East Lansing, MI: Author.

Insley, K. (1998). *Students' experiences in a constructivist classroom.* Unpublished doctoral dissertation, University of St. Thomas, St. Paul, MN.

Johnson, D., & Johnson, R. (1986). *Circles of learning: Cooperation in the classroom.* Edina, MN: Interaction Book Company.

Joyce, B., Weil, M., & Showers, B. (1992). *Models of teaching* (4th ed.). Needham Heights, MA: Allyn & Bacon.

Kegan, R. (1982). *The evolving self.* Cambridge, MA: Harvard University Press.

Kohn, A. (1996). *Beyond discipline.* Alexandria, VA: Association for Supervision and Curriculum Development.

Lakoff, G., & Johnson, M. (1980). *Metaphors we live by.* Chicago: University of Chicago Press.

Lambert, L., Dietz, M., Kent, K., Collay, M., & Richert, A. (1996) *Who will save our schools? Teachers as constructivist leaders.* Thousand Oaks, CA: Corwin.

Lambert, L., Walker, D., Zimmerman, D., Cooper, J., Lambert, M., Gardner, M., & Ford-Slack, P. J. (1995). *The constructivist leader.* New York: Teachers College Press.

Lewis, C. (1995). *Educating hearts and minds.* Cambridge, MA: Harvard University Press.

Little, J. W. (1990). Teachers as colleagues. In A. Lieberman (Ed.), *Schools as collaborative cultures: Creating the future now* (pp. 165-193). Bristol, PA: Falmer.

Morgan, G. (1997). *Images of organizations.* Thousand Oaks, CA: Sage.

National Board for Professional Teaching Standards. (1991). *Toward high and rigorous standards.* Detroit, MI: Author.

Peck, M. S. (1988). *The different drummer.* New York: Simon & Schuster.

Perkins, D. (1986). *Knowledge as design.* Hillsdale, NJ: Lawrence Erlbaum.

Perrone, V. (1991). *Expanding student assessment.* Alexandria, VA: Association for Supervision and Curriculum Development.

Perrow, C. (1984). *Normal accidents: Living with high-risk technologies.* New York: Basic Books.

Piaget, J. (1952). *The origins of intelligence in childhood.* New York: International Universities Press. (Original work published 1936)

Piaget, J. (1954). *The construction of reality in the child.* New York: Basic Books. (Original work published 1937)

Piaget, J. (1967). *Biology and knowledge.* Paris: Gallimard.

Piaget, J. (1974). *To understand is to invent.* New York: Grossman.

Progoff, I. (1992). *At a journal workshop: Writing to access the power of the unconscious and evoke creative ability.* New York: G. P. Putnam.

Rogoff, B., Matusov, E., & White, C. (1996). Models of teaching and learning: Participation in a community of learners. In D. Olson

& N. Torrance (Eds.), *The handbook of education and human development*. Cambridge, MA: Blackwell.

Schmuck, R., & Runkel, P. (1994). *The handbook of organization development in schools and colleges*. Prospect Heights, IL: Waveland.

Schmuck, R., & Schmuck, P. (1997). *Group processes in the classroom* (7th ed.). Madison, WI: Brown & Benchmark.

Schön, D. (1983). *The reflective practitioner: How professionals think in action*. New York: Basic Books.

Senge, P., & Kim, D. (1997, May). From fragmentation to integration: Building learning communities. *The Systems Thinker, 8*(4), 1-6.

Third International Mathematics and Science Study. (1997). *A splintered vision: An analysis of U.S. mathematics and science curricula*. Hingham, MA: Kluwer Academic Publishers Group.

Van Der Veer, R., & Valsiner, J. (1991). *Understanding Vygotsky: A quest for synthesis*. Cambridge, MA: Blackwell.

von Bertalanffy, L. (1973). *General systems theory*. New York: George Braziller.

von Glasersfeld, E. (1987). *The construction of knowledge: Contributions to conceptual semantics*. Seaside CA: Intersystems.

Vygotsky, L. S. (1987). *The collected works of L. S. Vygotsky. Vol. 1: Problems of general psychology* (N. Minick, Trans.). New York: Plenum.

Wolf, K., Whinery, B., & Hagerty, P. (1995). Teaching portfolios and portfolio conversations for teacher educators and teachers. *Action in Teacher Education, 17*(1), 30-39.

INDEX

Acting, 105-106
Apprenticeships, 124
Artifacts, cultural, 102-104
Arts and crafts activities, 43-44
Assessment, 79-81, 129
    authors' experiences, 76-77, 79-81, 91
    beliefs about, 81-82
    formative, 84-85
    of expectations, 11
    of learning circles, 85
    of teachers, 81-82
    peer, 87-89
    portfolios, 89-93
    program evaluation, 76-77
    purpose, 82-83
    relationship to expectations, 80
    replacing assumptions about, 83-84, 93-94
    scientific approach, 82
    selection of methods, 82-84, 87
    self-, 85-87
    summative, 84-85
    timing, 83

Basic schools, 25-26
Bianchi, Paul, 14
Blocks, wooden, 43
Bohm, D., 83
Boyer, E., 17, 18
Brosterman, N., 43
Building community. See Community

Capra, F., 7, 97

Child Development Project, 24
Clandinin, D. J., 57
Class projects, 125-126
Classrooms:
    as complex systems, 64
    building community in, 20, 21-22, 24
    climate, 50
    group processes, 50
    learning circles in, 123-127
Collay, Michelle, 35, 59-60
    personal experiences, 32, 49-50, 66-67, 91, 115
Communities of learners, xv, 131
    authors' experiences, xviii-xix, 54
    building, 17-18
    conditions for learning, xiii-xiv, 29-30, 114-117
    creating, 19-22, 118-121
    functions, 19
    governance, 26
    members, 18, 19
    relationship to learning circles, 3
    schools as, 17-18
    sustaining, 18
    See also Learning circles
Community:
    authors' experiences, 25-26
    autocratic structure, 23-24
    building, 9, 14, 19, 29-30, 129
    covenants, 20-21, 23
    definitions, 15
    democratic, 23, 24

evolution of, 16
in classrooms, 20, 21-22, 24
initiating, 19-22
maintaining, 22-23
metaphors for, 15
student projects in local, 124-125
sustaining, 23-26
traditions and rituals, 19
transforming, 26-29
Complex systems, 64
learning circles as, 15
representative theorists, 6, 7
Concordia Language Villages, 95-96
Conditions for learning, xiii-xiv, 8-12
assessing expectations, 11, 79-94, 129
building community, 9, 14-30, 129
changing cultures, 11, 95-96, 129-130
constructing knowledge, 9-10, 31-32, 129
correspondence with constructivist learning design, 123
documenting reflection, 10-11, 64, 72-78, 129
in classrooms, 123-127
re-creating, 114-117
supporting learners, 10, 47-50, 52, 129
Constructing knowledge. See Knowledge
Constructivist collaborations, 59-60
Constructivist learning, 15, 32-35
curriculum development, 27-29
examples, 35-42
representative theorists, 6, 7
value, 44-46, 94
Constructivist learning design, 35-39, 123
Covenants, 20-21, 23, 110-111
CREED (activities of cultures), 98-101
Csikszentmihalyi, M., 7, 82
Cultures:
acting as method of learning about, 105-106
adult, in schools, 50-51

analyzing in learning circles, 101-102
artifacts, 102-104
as interdependent networks, 96-97
authors' experiences, 95-96, 104-106
changing, 11, 95-96, 129-130
classroom, 50
dance in, 104-105
definitions, 97-98
leadership in, 108-110
of schools, 95, 99-101
rules about activities, 98-101
transformation of, 102, 107
understanding, 97-101
Curriculum development, 27-29, 56-57, 67

Dance, 104-105
DeGeus, A., 7, 15
Democracy, 23, 24
Dietz, M., 59-60
Dizney, Henry, 32
Documenting reflection. See Reflection
Duckworth, E., 57
Dunlap, Diane, personal experiences, 48, 57, 76-77, 79-81, 105-106
Duras, M., 105

Education reform, xvi-xvii, 127-129
Emory University, 13
Enloe, Walter, 125
personal experiences, 13-14, 21-22, 25-26, 95-96, 104-105
Evaluation. See Assessment

Flow, 82-83
See also Optimal experience
Folding paper exercise, 39-41
Ford-Slack, P. J., 76
Formative evaluation, 84-85
Freire, P., 114
Froebel, Friedrich, 43
Fullan, M., 18

Gagnon, George W., Jr., 35
personal experiences, 1-2, 54, 62-63, 91
Goodlad, J., 24
Group processes, 15
in classrooms, 50
learning in small groups, 51-53
representative theorists, 6, 7

Hagerty, P., 89
Hands Across Seas project, 22
Holding environments, 96-97
Hollingsworth, S., 57
Human development, 33
analogy to learning circles, 7
dimensions, 3, 12
object relations, 42

Implicate order, theory of, 83-84
In-service education, xiv, 23, 55
Insley, K., 27
Intelligence, 33-34
Interdependent networks, 6, 7, 96-97

Johnson, M., 69
Journals, 67-68, 72-73

Kegan, R., 7, 96-97
Kent, K., 59-60
Kim, D., 16, 111
Kindergarten, 43-44
Knowledge:
constructing, 9-10, 31-32, 44-46, 129
dimensions of, 39
relationship to environment, 34
See also Constructivist learning
Kohn, A., 24

Lakoff, G., 69
Lambert, L., 59-60, 97
Language. *See* Metaphors
Leadership:
by teachers, 112-113
definition, 108
in learning circles, xvi, 109-112, 113

in schools, 108-109
Learning:
as optimal experience, 82-83
as play, 79
authors' experiences, 1-2, 13-14, 21-22
children teaching adults, 41
conditions for, 8-12
definition, 3, 18, 33
dimensions of human development, 3, 12
in small groups, 51-53
physical, sensory, and communicative, 45
social aspects, xiii-xiv, 47
students' process of, 35
styles, 41
supporting. *See* Support for learners
Learning circles, 2-3
advantages of small groups, xv-xvii, 51-53
assessment. *See* Assessment
authors' experiences, 47-50, 57, 114-115
developing, 17-18, 116-117, 118-121
developmental phases, 129-130
ecological analogy, 7-8
education reform influenced by, xvi-xvii
effectiveness, 51
examples in schools, 56-57
forming, 19-20
individual goals in, 65, 85, 86
initiating, 118
leaders, xvi, 109-112, 113
maintaining, 118-119
meeting times, 119
members, 2-3, 29-30, 51
need for variety of, 18-19
practical considerations, 118-121
precursor ideas, 122-123
purposes, 2-3, 51, 55-57, 60, 114
relationship to communities of learners, 3, 29-30, 53
research purposes, 57-60

roles of individuals, 120
structures, 34-35
sustaining, 119-120
theoretical basis, 5-8
transforming, 120-121
variations, 121
Learning covenants. *See* Covenants
Living organizations:
    as metaphor for learning com-
        munities, 15, 118
    processes, 12
    representative theorists, 6-7
    schools as, 15-16

MAPS (models, arguments, pur-
    poses, and structures), 75-76
Mathematics, bases lesson, 36-38
Mentors, students as, 59
Mentorship, in learning circles, 106-
    108
Metaphors:
    as reflection technique, 69-72
    for community, 15
    for learning circles, 109, 118
Minneapolis Public Schools, 91
Morgan, G., 15

National Board for Professional
    Teaching Standards
    (NBPTS), xiii, 60, 131
NBPTS. *See* National Board for Pro-
    fessional Teaching Standards
Normal accidents, 64

Object relations, 42
Optimal experience, 6, 7, 15, 82-83
Organization development, 50
    See also Group processes
Origami, 39-41

Paideia School (Atlanta), 13-14
Paper, folding, 39-41
Peck, M. S., 16
Peer assessment, xvii, 87-89
Perkins, D., 75
Perrone, V., 54, 90
Perrow, C., 7, 64

Piaget, J., 6-7, 15, 32, 33, 34, 42
Play, 79
"Playing Baby" exercise, 42
Portfolios:
    authors' experiences, 91
    developing, 89, 90-92
    discussing in learning circles, 89-
        90
    purpose, 89, 90
    reflection on, 73-74
    value of, 92-93
Preservice teachers, 54-55
Professional development:
    activities, 22-23
    distinction from staff develop-
        ment, xiv
    in schools, 66
    individual goals, 64-67, 85, 86
    individualized, 55
    learning circles for, 55-57
    theoretical foundation, 5-8
Progoff, I., 67
Program evaluation, 76-77
Proudfoot, Rob, 67

Rainbow Blocks, 36
Reflection, 62
    authors' experiences, 62-63, 66-
        67
    documenting, 10-11, 64, 74-75,
        77, 129
    forms, 63-64
    journals, 67-68, 72-73
    learning circle activities, 73, 74-
        75, 77-78
    metaphor use, 69-72
    on portfolios, 73-74
    on professional development
        goals, 64-67
    program evaluation by, 76-77
    stepping-stone stories, 67-68
    structured, 74-76
    value of documenting, 62-63,
        64, 68
    with colleagues, 73-74
Reform, educational. *See* Education
    reform

Research, learning circles for, 57-60
Richert, A., 59-60
Runkel, P., 7, 19, 48, 49, 50

Schmuck, P., 7, 50
Schmuck, R., 7, 19, 48, 49, 50
Schon, D., 63, 78
School districts, cultural changes, 127-129
Schools:
  as complex systems, 64
  as learning communities, 17-18
  as living organizations, 15-16
  basic, 25-26
  community projects, 124-125
  cultural changes, 127
  cultures, 50-51, 95, 99-101
  flexible groupings of students, 18-19
  international partnerships, 22
  leadership in, 108-109
  professional development in, 66
  student mentors, 59
  See also Classrooms
Self-assessment, 85-87
Senge, P., 16, 111
Service learning projects, 124
Staff development, xiv, 23, 55
Stepping-stone stories, 67-68
Students:
  as mentors, 59
  learning processes, 35
  See also Classrooms; Schools
Summative evaluation, 84-85
Support for learners, 10, 47-50, 129
  in learning circles, 52
  preservice teachers, 54-55

Systems thinking, 64
  See also Complex systems

TAWL. *See* Teachers Applying Whole Language
Teacher support teams, xvii
Teachers:
  as leaders, 112-113
  as mentors, 107
  creating conditions for communities of learners, 115-117
  evaluation of, 81-82
  metaphors for roles, 69-72
  peer support, 55
  preservice, 54-55
  professional support groups, 58-59
  professionalism, xiv, 69
  roles, 31-32, 69-72
  value of learning circles for new, 49
  See also Classrooms; Professional development
Teachers Applying Whole Language (TAWL), 58
Teaching, definition, 33
Third International Math and Science Study (TIMSS), 38
TIMSS. *See* Third International Math and Science Study

von Bertalanffy, L., 7, 64
von Glasersfeld, E., 7, 33
Vygotsky, L. S., 7, 33

Whinery, B., 89
Whole-part relations, 34, 112
Wolf, K., 89

CORWIN
PRESS

The Corwin Press logo—a raven striding across an open book—represents the happy union of courage and learning. We are a professional-level publisher of books and journals for K–12 educators, and we are committed to creating and providing resources that embody these qualities. Corwin's motto is "Success for All Learners."